MongoDB High Availability

Design and implement a highly available server using the latest features of MongoDB

Afshin Mehrabani

BIRMINGHAM - MUMBAI

MongoDB High Availability

First published: July 2014

Production reference: 1170714

Published by Packt Publishing Ltd.

Livery Place
35 Livery Street
Birmingham B3 2PB, UK.

ISBN 978-1-78398-672-9

www.packtpub.com

Cover image by Zarko Piljak (zpiljak@gmail.com)

Credits

Author
Afshin Mehrabani

Reviewers
Pierre-Louis Gottfrois
Jason Nichols
Laurence Putra
Khaled Tannir

Commissioning Editor
Taron Pereira

Acquisition Editor
Neha Nagwekar

Content Development Editor
Athira Laji

Technical Editor
Akash Rajiv Sharma

Copy Editors
Alisha Aranha
Roshni Banerjee
Sarang Chari
Stuti Srivastava

Project Coordinators
Melita Lobo
Harshal Ved

Proofreaders
Ameesha Green
Paul Hindle

Indexer
Tejal Soni

Graphics
Sheetal Aute

Production Coordinator
Alwin Roy

Cover Work
Alwin Roy

About the Author

Afshin Mehrabani is an open source programmer. He is studying to be a computer software engineer. He started programming and web development when he was 12 years old, as well as starting with PHP. Later, he joined the Iran Technical and Vocational Training Organization. He secured the first place and received a gold medal in a competition which was conducted across the entire country in the area of web development. He became a member of the Iran National Foundation of Elite after producing a variety of new programming ideas.

He was a software engineer at the Tehran Stock Exchange and is now the head of the web development team in the Yara Company. He cofounded the Usablica team in early 2012 to develop and produce usable applications. He is the author of IntroJs, WideArea, flood.js and some other open source projects.

He has contributed to Socket.IO, Engine.IO, and some other open source projects. He is also interested in creating and contributing to open source applications, writing programming articles, and challenging himself with new programming technologies.

He has written different articles about JavaScript, Node.js, HTML5, and MongoDB that have been published on different academic websites. Afshin has 5 years of experience in PHP, Python, C#, JavaScript, HTML5, and Node.js in many financial and stock trading projects.

I would like to thank my parents and my lovely sister, Parvin, for their support, which gave me the power to keep going.

About the Reviewers

Pierre-Louis Gottfrois is a full stack web developer who loves to write decoupled and well-tested applications. Fascinated by innovations, he is always ready to face new challenges. He is currently working on Ruby on Rails with great mentors such as Benjamin Roth, one of the top researchers on StackOverflow. Learning quickly and always paying attention to details, he is skillful but is also a great person to grab a beer with.

Jason Nichols is an expert in financial and econometric modeling and developing real-time data-visualization apps. With more than 15 years of JavaScript experience and numerous certifications and licenses in both software development and finance, Jason is a leading authority in applying JavaScript to complex real-time data analytics.

Laurence Putra is a software engineer working in Singapore and runs the annual GeekcampSG. He also runs the Singapore MongoDB User Group. In his free time, he hacks away at random stuff and picks up new technologies. His key interests lie in security and distributed systems. For more information, view his profile at geeksphere.net.

Khaled Tannir has been working with computers since 1980. He has a Bachelor's degree in Electronics and a Master's degree in System Information Architectures, and completed his education with a Master's degree in research.

He is a Microsoft Certified Solutions Developer (MCSD), and is an experienced Solution Architect with more than 20 years of technical experience in leading the development and implementation of software solutions and giving technical presentations for many companies in France and Canada.

An avid technologist, he has focused on Big Data technologies since 2010. Currently, he is working as a Big Data architect lead and trainer for a large financial institution in Canada.

Khaled is the author of *RavenDB 2.x Beginner's Guide* and *Optimizing Hadoop for MapReduce*, both books by Packt Publishing. He was also a technical reviewer for *Pentaho Analytics for MongoDB, Bo Borland, Packt Publishing*.

He enjoys taking landscape and night photos, travelling, playing video games, creating funny electronics gadgets with Arduino / .NET Gadgeteer, and of course spending time with his wife and family. You can contact him at contact@khaledtannir.net.

www.PacktPub.com

Support files, eBooks, discount offers, and more

You might want to visit www.PacktPub.com for support files and downloads related to your book.

Did you know that Packt offers eBook versions of every book published, with PDF and ePub files available? You can upgrade to the eBook version at www.PacktPub.com and as a print book customer, you are entitled to a discount on the eBook copy. Get in touch with us at service@packtpub.com for more details.

At www.PacktPub.com, you can also read a collection of free technical articles, sign up for a range of free newsletters and receive exclusive discounts and offers on Packt books and eBooks.

http://PacktLib.PacktPub.com

Do you need instant solutions to your IT questions? PacktLib is Packt's online digital book library. Here, you can access, read and search across Packt's entire library of books.

Why subscribe?

- Fully searchable across every book published by Packt
- Copy and paste, print and bookmark content
- On demand and accessible via web browser

Free access for Packt account holders

If you have an account with Packt at www.PacktPub.com, you can use this to access PacktLib today and view nine entirely free books. Simply use your login credentials for immediate access.

Table of Contents

Preface

Before the invention of NoSQL, almost all databases were structural. This means that developers had to define the structure of the database before using it. Despite all the benefits of using this approach, sometimes, following such a method came with issues. For instance, you couldn't (or at least it was difficult to) have schemaless data.

Later, the NoSQL concept and all the technologies related to it were invented to rescue programmers.

The following sections show a brief history of the term NoSQL, which is taken from `http://en.wikipedia.org/wiki/NoSQL`.

> *"Carlo Strozzi used the term NoSQL in 1998 to name his lightweight, open source relational database that did not expose the standard SQL interface."*

NoSQL databases are classified in the following ways:

- Column (HBase, Cassandra)
- Document (MongoDB, Couchbase)
- Key-value (Redis, Riak, MemcacheDB)
- Graph (Neo4j, OrientDB)

Have a look at the following image:

So, why use NoSQL instead of relational databases? There are many different opinions about the benefits of relational or non-relational databases, but to give you the gist of all conversations, the following are the major reasons to use NoSQL:

- A more flexible data model and a dynamic schema
- Scalability
- Better efficiency and performance

Compared to relational database systems, NoSQL databases have a remarkable feature that enables developers to change the data model after inserting data; that is, developers can insert data without defining the data model. This comes in handy when you have a data model that might change after data is inserted.

One of the great NoSQL database facilities is scaling. Almost all NoSQL technologies support a built-in mechanism to scale a database horizontally, and not vertically. Auto-sharding is responsible for this task.

Additionally, NoSQL databases support integrated caching, which improves the read/write performances of a database. The database will frequently use data in memory and restore them while reading data, but not from the disk. This method will affect database performance and improve the overall database speed when reading and writing data.

MongoDB is one of the pioneers in implementing the NoSQL concept by using "Document" as the infrastructure when saving and restoring data from a database. MongoDB is a cross-platform, document-oriented database system. MongoDB was developed by 10gen, a software company, in October 2007. The latest stable version of MongoDB is 2.4.9, and was released on January 10, 2014.

MongoDB is the leading NoSQL database, with stunning implementation, and it has a vibrant community. As you know, one of the basic reasons to choose a technology is an active and lively community so there is always someone who can help you and answer your questions. The graph, shown in the following screenshot is taken from `http://www.mongodb.com/leading-nosql-database`:

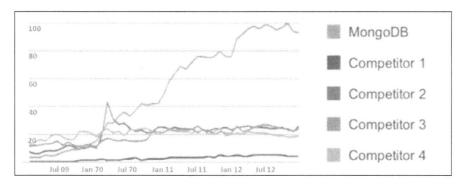

You can ask your questions in StackOverflow or on their individual forums, and you will get an answer at the earliest. Furthermore, there are various books and articles available about MongoDB.

Here, we have some remarkable features of MongoDB:

- **Schemaless data**: Developers are able to store any data model or change the schema during or after inserting data.

- **Replication**: MongoDB provides high availability with replica sets. A replica set contains two or more copies of data, and each one can be either primary or secondary.

- **Load balancing**: Using sharding, MongoDB can scale horizontally, so data will split between two ranges based on sharding keys.

- **File storage**: MongoDB has a feature that is called GridFS, so you can use MongoDB as a filesystem to store and load data from the disk.

In this book, we will discuss remedies and solutions to provide a highly available MongoDB server. First of all, we will go through the problems and issues that cause server downtime, such as errors or server crashes. In the next chapters, by introducing remedies and exploring the problem with a real-world example, we will sort out the issues.

What this book covers

Chapter 1, Understanding the MongoDB Architecture and Processes, discusses the MongoDB architecture, its processes, and binary files such as, mongos or mongod.

Chapter 2, Understanding MongoDB's Failures and Limitations, covers MongoDB's failures, such as server downtime, errors while inserting or reading, and so on. Also, we discuss the solutions to cover and reduce downtime.

Chapter 3, Clustering in MongoDB, provides an overview of MongoDB clustering solutions in a production environment.

Chapter 4, Utilizing a Replica Set, covers replica sets and explains the basic concepts of this feature.

Chapter 5, Replica Set in Action, introduces real-world examples using replica sets to provide high availability for the server.

Chapter 6, Understanding the Concept of Sharding, explains the understanding and utilization of the sharding feature in MongoDB.

Chapter 7, Sharding in Action, explains the use of sharding in action, to enable clustering in an existing MongoDB database and even in a new one.

Chapter 8, Analyzing and Improving Database Performance, covers using the latest MongoDB features to boost the reading and writing performance.

Chapter 9, Migrating Instances and Reducing Downtime, teaches the database migrations and solutions to reduce server downtime.

Chapter 10, Monitoring and Troubleshooting the Database, discusses tools and techniques to manage database performance and uptime. Also, this includes a discussion on the ways to troubleshoot database problems.

What you need for this book

Since MongoDB is cross-platform, you can use all operating systems, including Linux, Windows, or Mac OS X.

In this book, we need the latest version of MongoDB. Currently, the latest stable version is 2.6.1, and you can download it from the official MongoDB website.

Who this book is for

The *MongoDB High Availability* book is a complete manual to use MongoDB in the production environment.

If you need to use MongoDB in production or you are interested to learn about clustering solutions in MongoDB, this book is the right choice. With this step-by-step guide, you can enable features for your database easily and follow the instructions to use the available methods. Familiarity with MongoDB is expected for you to understand the content of this book.

Conventions

In this book, you will find a number of styles of text that distinguish between different kinds of information. Here are some examples of these styles, and an explanation of their meaning.

Code words in text, database table names, folder names, filenames, file extensions, pathnames, dummy URLs, user input, and Twitter handles are shown as follows: "In the MongoDB structure, the mongo file is responsible for this task."

A block of code is set as follows:

```
{
    "_id": ObjectId("725c211a412f812548cv3258"),
    "data": 1
}
```

Any command-line input or output is written as follows:

```
-f (file size): unlimited
-t (cpu time): unlimited
-v (virtual memory): unlimited
-n (open files): 64000
-m (memory size): unlimited
-u (processes/threads): 32000
```

New terms and **important words** are shown in bold. Words that you see on the screen, in menus or dialog boxes for example, appear in the text like this: "MMS supports all types of MongoDB instances, including **Sharded Cluster**, **Standalone**, **Replica Set**, and **Master/Slave**."

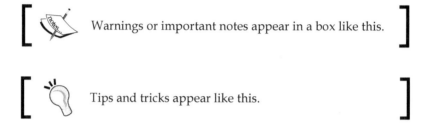

Warnings or important notes appear in a box like this.

Tips and tricks appear like this.

Reader feedback

Feedback from our readers is always welcome. Let us know what you think about this book—what you liked or may have disliked. Reader feedback is important for us to develop titles that you really get the most out of.

To send us general feedback, simply send an e-mail to feedback@packtpub.com, and mention the book title via the subject of your message.

If there is a topic that you have expertise in and you are interested in either writing or contributing to a book, see our author guide on www.packtpub.com/authors.

Customer support

Now that you are the proud owner of a Packt book, we have a number of things to help you to get the most from your purchase.

Errata

Although we have taken every care to ensure the accuracy of our content, mistakes do happen. If you find a mistake in one of our books—maybe a mistake in the text or the code—we would be grateful if you would report this to us. By doing so, you can save other readers from frustration and help us improve subsequent versions of this book. If you find any errata, please report them by visiting http://www.packtpub.com/submit-errata, selecting your book, clicking on the **errata submission form** link, and entering the details of your errata. Once your errata are verified, your submission will be accepted and the errata will be uploaded on our website, or added to any list of existing errata, under the Errata section of that title. Any existing errata can be viewed by selecting your title from http://www.packtpub.com/support.

Piracy

Piracy of copyright material on the Internet is an ongoing problem across all media. At Packt, we take the protection of our copyright and licenses very seriously. If you come across any illegal copies of our works, in any form, on the Internet, please provide us with the location address or website name immediately so that we can pursue a remedy.

Please contact us at copyright@packtpub.com with a link to the suspected pirated material.

We appreciate your help in protecting our authors, and our ability to bring you valuable content.

Questions

You can contact us at questions@packtpub.com if you are having a problem with any aspect of the book, and we will do our best to address it.

1
Understanding the MongoDB Architecture and Processes

To be able to diagnose a MongoDB server or change the default preferences to provide better performance in a database, we need to understand the primitive MongoDB settings and management tools. MongoDB consists of binary files and services that make the infrastructure of the server, and each file performs a specific task.

In this chapter, we will go through the MongoDB processes to discover why they exist and what each process does exactly.

Utilizing MongoDB components

This section contains a brief description of the MongoDB components, file names, and the main purpose of each of them. We will further discuss each item in detail. The following diagram shows you the four main components of MongoDB:

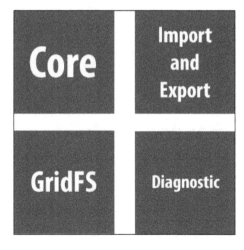

MongoDB components can mainly be classified into the following categories:

- Core components
- Import and export tools
- Diagnostic tools
- File storage (GridFS) tools

Each file can be placed into one of the aforementioned categories. The core component files are used to run the MongoDB server and start it. The files are also used to manage the MongoDB server from the command-line interface or manage clustering tasks.

Using import and export tools, developers can create dump files from their database in different formats such as BSON, JSON or CSV and restore them into another database again. Certain tools are used to create or restore BSON files, and some tools are responsible for generating and importing other common formats such as JSON or CSV.

MongoDB has many built-in diagnostic tools to manage and control the currently running server. Finally, we can use GridFS tools to interact with filesystem and GridFS components. In the next section, we will give you more details for each category and the processes inside them.

Understanding the core components

Inside this category, you can find the core processes that are required to start the MongoDB server. The MongoDB engine uses these tools to accept requests from different clients.

The components and executable files in this group are as follows:

- mongod
- mongo
- mongos

Understanding mongod

The mongod component is the primary process that is needed for MongoDB to start the server. It manages requests or queries and handles connections.

The following screenshot is the result of executing `mongod` from the command-line interface:

```
sh-3.2# mongod
mongod --help for help and startup options
Fri Mar  7 17:19:01 [initandlisten] MongoDB starting : pid=5613 port=27017 dbpath=/data/db/ 64-bi
t host=Afshin-Mehrabanis-MacBook-Pro-5.local
Fri Mar  7 17:19:01 [initandlisten] db version v2.0.0, pdfile version 4.5
Fri Mar  7 17:19:01 [initandlisten] git version: 695c67dff0ffc361b8568a13366f027caa406222
Fri Mar  7 17:19:01 [initandlisten] build info: Darwin erh2.10gen.cc 9.6.0 Darwin Kernel Version
9.6.0: Mon Nov 24 17:37:00 PST 2008; root:xnu-1228.9.59~1/RELEASE_I386 i386 BOOST_LIB_VERSION=1_4
0
Fri Mar  7 17:19:01 [initandlisten] options: {}
Fri Mar  7 17:19:01 [initandlisten] journal dir=/data/db/journal
Fri Mar  7 17:19:01 [initandlisten] recover : no journal files present, no recovery needed
Fri Mar  7 17:19:01 [websvr] admin web console waiting for connections on port 28017
Fri Mar  7 17:19:01 [initandlisten] waiting for connections on port 27017
```

The preceding screenshot illustrates the result of running `mongod` from the command line, that is, you finally have a MongoDB server running on port 27017 and a web interface on port 28017, which is the default port.

Like other MongoDB commands, in order to see the parameters of the `mongod` process, you can simply run following command:

`mongod --help`

Here, you can see the result of running the `mongod` command with the `--help` parameter. This is shown in the following screenshot:

```
sh-3.2# mongod --help
Allowed options:

General options:
  -h [ --help ]               show this usage information
  --version                   show version information
  -f [ --config ] arg         configuration file specifying additional options
  -v [ --verbose ]            be more verbose (include multiple times for more
                              verbosity e.g. -vvvvv)
  --quiet                     quieter output
  --port arg                  specify port number
  --bind_ip arg               comma separated list of ip addresses to listen on
                              - all local ips by default
  --maxConns arg              max number of simultaneous connections
  --objcheck                  inspect client data for validity on receipt
  --logpath arg               log file to send write to instead of stdout - has
                              to be a file, not directory
  --logappend                 append to logpath instead of over-writing
  --pidfilepath arg           full path to pidfile (if not set, no pidfile is
                              created)
  --keyFile arg               private key for cluster authentication (only for
                              replica sets)
  --nounixsocket              disable listening on unix sockets
  --unixSocketPrefix arg      alternative directory for UNIX domain sockets
                              (defaults to /tmp)
  --fork                      fork server process
  --auth                      run with security
  --cpu                       periodically show cpu and iowait utilization
  --dbpath arg                directory for datafiles
  --diaglog arg               0=off 1=W 2=R 3=both 7=W+some reads
  --directoryperdb            each database will be stored in a separate
                              directory
```

To read more about the command and figure out what each parameter does, you can visit the MongoDB documentation page at http://docs.mongodb.org/manual/reference/program/mongod/.

Utilizing mongo

After starting the database server, we need to interact with it to issue a command, run commands, run queries, or get reports. In the MongoDB structure, the mongo file is responsible for this task. This is an interactive JavaScript shell that you can utilize from your command-line environment.

Using this executable file, database administrators and also developers can manage the database server or get available databases and collections.

The following screenshot is the result of running the mongo command:

```
➜  /etc  mongo
MongoDB shell version: 2.6.0
connecting to: test
```

Fortunately, the mongo component provides internal help so that developers can use it to get more information for each command.

The following screenshot shows you the result of running the help command:

```
> help
        db.help()                    help on db methods
        db.mycoll.help()             help on collection methods
        sh.help()                    sharding helpers
        rs.help()                    replica set helpers
        help admin                   administrative help
        help connect                 connecting to a db help
        help keys                    key shortcuts
        help misc                    misc things to know
        help mr                      mapreduce

        show dbs                     show database names
        show collections            show collections in current database
        show users                   show users in current database
        show profile                 show most recent system.profile entries with time >= 1ms
        show logs                    show the accessible logger names
        show log [name]              prints out the last segment of log in memory, 'global' is default
        use <db_name>                set current database
        db.foo.find()                list objects in collection foo
        db.foo.find( { a : 1 } )     list objects in foo where a == 1
        it                           result of the last line evaluated; use to further iterate
        DBQuery.shellBatchSize = x   set default number of items to display on shell
        exit                         quit the mongo shell
>
```

To acquire more information about MongoDB and all its parameters, you can visit the MongoDB documentation page at http://docs.mongodb.org/manual/reference/program/mongo/.

Learning about mongos

The mongos instance is responsible for routing read/write commands to shards in a sharded cluster. In fact, all processes and applications will connect to this instance and run queries, then the mongos instance will route commands to available shards. The applications will not interact with shards directly. To run the mongos instance, we can provide sharded cluster configurations using a config file or command-line parameters.

In further chapters, we will discuss this process in detail.

 To gain more knowledge about the mongos command and its parameters, you can visit the MongoDB documentation page at http://docs.mongodb.org/manual/reference/program/mongos/.

Import and export tools

The tools in this group are used to export or restore files from the database. Mainly, components in this category are classified into two different groups. This includes components that work with binary data or interact with common data formats such as JSON, CSV, and so on.

Using import and export tools

In order to import or export binary data from and into the database, developers can use tools in this group. We use tools and utilities in this category to create or restore backups for our MongoDB server. In further chapters, we will discuss the backup strategies in detail.

The following are the tools that are available to perform these kinds of tasks:

* mongodump
* mongorestore
* bsondump
* mongooplog

Understanding mongodump

This process comes in handy when developers or system administrators want to create a dump file from a database in the binary format. This utility and other related tools are useful for MongoDB backup strategies.

The mongodump process is able to retrieve data from either mongod or mongos processes.

 For more information on mongodump, visit the MongoDB documentation page at http://docs.mongodb.org/manual/reference/program/mongodump/.

Utilizing mongorestore

This process is used to restore and write the binary files that are generated by the mongodump process into the database server. To restore data, mongorestore can establish a new database or use an existing database. Just like the mongodump instance, mongorestore can connect to a mongos instance or it can connect directly to the mongod process.

 To read more about mongostore, you can visit the MongoDB documentation page at http://docs.mongodb.org/manual/reference/program/mongorestore/.

Learning about bsondump

The bsondump process is used to convert the BSON format data to common data formats such as JSON. Essentially, bsondump comes in handy when developers want to convert dump files that are generated by mongodump to human-readable formats.

A very simple usage of this command is shown in the following command line:

```
bsondump data.bson>data.json
```

Understanding mongooplog

The mongooplog is a utility that duplicates oplog from one server to another server, for instance, in order to perform a migration task. In order to perform the migration operation, mongooplog accepts two parameters, the from and to server addresses.

What is oplog?

The `oplog` or operation log is a capped collection (a fixed-sized collection) of data that keeps the record of all data altering operations. In further chapters, we will explain this feature in detail.

The following is a simple usage of this command:

```
mongooplog --from server1 --host server2
```

The preceding command line will connect to the MongoDB instance of `server1` and copy the entire `oplog` to `server2` instance.

Using data tools

In this group, we have two utilities that help us generate or import data in human-readable formats such as JSON or CSV into or from the MongoDB instance. These are mentioned in the following lists:

- `mongoimport`
- `mongoexport`

Understanding mongoexport

In order to export data in JSON or CSV formats from the MongoDB instance, developers can use this utility.

The following is a simple usage of this command:

```
mongoexport --db mydb --collection posts --out export.json
```

The preceding command line will connect to a local instance of MongoDB, retrieve all records from the `posts` collection of the `mydb` database in the JSON format, and write all outputs to the `export.json` file.

Utilizing mongoimport

The `mongoimport` utility can help you import the produced export files in JSON, CSV or TSV formats into the MongoDB instance. The export files can be generated from either `mongoexport` or from other third-party export tools.

The following example is a basic usage of this command:

```
mongoimport --db mydb --collection posts --file export.json
```

The preceding command line will import the `export.json` entries into the `posts` collection of the `mydb` database. The same instruction can be used for other data formats using the `--type` option.

Diagnostic tools

One of the important tools of a database system is diagnostic tools. Fortunately, MongoDB has built-in diagnostic tools that enable developers to diagnose the server or get a brief report from the system.

We have the following utilities placed in this group:

- `mongostat`
- `mongotop`
- `mongosniff`
- `mongoperf`

In the next sections, you can read a brief description of each utility.

Learning about mongostat

This tool produces a brief summary of relevant statistics of the currently running MongoDB instances, either the `mongod` or `mongos` instance.

The following screenshot illustrates the output of this tool:

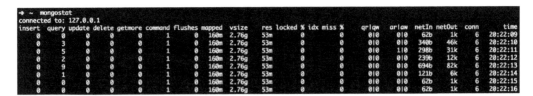

The preceding screenshot shows you the number of queries, update, insert, and delete operations from the database every second.

The following bullet list gives you a brief description for each column:

- `insert`: This refers to the number of insert operations per second.
- `query`: This refers to the number of queries per second.
- `update`: This refers to the number of update operations per second.
- `delete`: This refers to the number of delete operations per second.

- getmore: This refers to the number of getmore operations (that is, the it command in mongo shell) per second.

- command: This refers to the number of executed commands since the last mongostat call.

- flushes: This refers to the number of fsync operations at the time of the last mongostat execution. The fsync operation is a system call that flushes all dirty in-memory pages to the disk.

- mapped: This refers to the total amount of data mapped in megabytes.

- vsize: This refers to the amount of virtual memory in megabytes used by the process at the time of the last mongostat execution.

- res: This refers to the amount of resident memory in megabytes used by the process at the time of the last mongostat execution.

- locked: This refers to the percentage of time in a global write lock.

- idx miss: This refers to the percentage of index access attempts that required a page fault.

- qr: This refers to the number of clients in the queue that are waiting for read operations.

- qw: This refers to the number of clients in the queue that are waiting for write operations.

- ar: This refers to the number of clients that execute read operations.

- aw: This refers to the number of clients that execute write operations.

- netIn: This refers to the traffic received by the MongoDB instance in bytes.

- netOut: This refers to the traffic sent by the MongoDB instance in bytes.

- conn: This refers to the current total option connections.

The refresh interval can be changed using the following command:

```
mongostat [options] [sleep time]
```

Utilizing mongotop

The mongotop utility provides you with a mechanism to get information about time spent on read/write operations. This command is similar to Unix's top command.

The following screenshot shows you a simple usage of `mongotop`:

ns	total	read	write	2014-05-17T18:07:03
testdb.testcollection	372ms	372ms	0ms	
testdb.system.profile	0ms	0ms	0ms	
testdb.system.namespaces	0ms	0ms	0ms	
testdb.system.indexes	0ms	0ms	0ms	
sourcedoc.users	0ms	0ms	0ms	
sourcedoc.userorganizations	0ms	0ms	0ms	
sourcedoc.system.namespaces	0ms	0ms	0ms	
sourcedoc.system.indexes	0ms	0ms	0ms	
ns	total	read	write	2014-05-17T18:07:04
testdb.testcollection	0ms	0ms	0ms	
testdb.system.profile	0ms	0ms	0ms	
testdb.system.namespaces	0ms	0ms	0ms	
testdb.system.indexes	0ms	0ms	0ms	
sourcedoc.users	0ms	0ms	0ms	
sourcedoc.userorganizations	0ms	0ms	0ms	
sourcedoc.system.namespaces	0ms	0ms	0ms	
sourcedoc.system.indexes	0ms	0ms	0ms	
ns	total	read	write	2014-05-17T18:07:05
testdb.testcollection	385ms	385ms	0ms	
testdb.system.profile	0ms	0ms	0ms	
testdb.system.namespaces	0ms	0ms	0ms	
testdb.system.indexes	0ms	0ms	0ms	
sourcedoc.users	0ms	0ms	0ms	
sourcedoc.userorganizations	0ms	0ms	0ms	
sourcedoc.system.namespaces	0ms	0ms	0ms	
sourcedoc.system.indexes	0ms	0ms	0ms	

Understanding mongosniff

The `mongosniff` is a tool that is used to fetch live MongoDB collection statistics. While inserting or querying data from the MongoDB instances, you can run the `mongosniff` command and connect it to your MongoDB instance to see what the database does.

 Please note that in order to use this utility, you should install the `libpcap` library first. To install the `libpcap` library, please visit its official website at `http://www.tcpdump.org/#documentation`.

A simple usage of the `mongosniff` tool is as follows:

```
sudo mongosniff  --source NET lo0
```

The preceding command line will listen to the loopback interface (localhost). This interface is `lo0` in Mac OS systems and `lo` for other operating systems, usually. You can get the list for your network interfaces using the `ifconfig` command. If you're using Windows as the operating system, you can get the list of network interfaces using the following command:

```
ipconfig /all
```

Utilizing mongoperf

The `mongoperf` tool represents the disk I/O performance. It checks the I/O in a specified interval and illustrates it. This utility can be used independent of MongoDB.

File storage (GridFS) tools

With the help of GridFS, MongoDB can be used as a filesystem. The processes in this section are used to manage and control the GridFS feature.

There is one process in this category, which is as follows:

* `mongofiles`

Understanding mongofiles

This utility enables developers to retrieve files that are stored in the database in the GridFS collection. The `mongofiles` utility come in handy when developers need to interact with files stored in the database from the command-line environment.

The usage of this command looks like the following:

```
mongofiles <options> <commands> <filename>
```

The following example is a simple usage of this utility:

```
mongofiles -d mydb list
```

The preceding command line will retrieve all files in the GridFS collection from the `mydb` database.

 For more information on `mongofiles`, please visit the MongoDB documentation page at `http://docs.mongodb.org/manual/reference/program/mongofiles/`.

Summary

In this chapter, we went through basic MongoDB topics such as major MongoDB processes, how they work, and why they exist.

We learned that MongoDB consists of some main components such as core, import and export, GridFS, and diagnostic tools. Then, we discussed the basic processes that make MongoDB work, that is, `mongod` and `mongos`. Also, we learned that developers or system administrators can manage MongoDB using the `mongo` process. This is an interactive JavaScript shell, which enables developers to run and execute commands, queries, and administration procedures.

Next, we talked about import and export tools that give developers the ability to export and import objects from and into the database, which is used for backup and restoration procedures. In addition, you can find a brief description of the GridFS components and diagnostic tools that are required to work with the filesystem. We also learned how to find database statistics and issues with diagnostic tools.

In the next chapter, we will learn about the causes of failure in MongoDB and find remedies and solutions to overcome these problems.

2
Understanding MongoDB's Failures and Limitations

As you are undoubtedly aware, developers might face data loss or server failures while working with the server, just like other database engines. This book is aimed at providing you with solutions so that you have a readily available database engine in MongoDB. Before talking about the remedies, you should understand the main reasons for failures and limitations.

In this chapter, we will understand the reasons for MongoDB's failures and limitations in the production environment.

Understanding the limitation of a 32-bit version of MongoDB

If you want to deploy MongoDB in a production environment, it's necessary that you use a 64-bit version and not a 32-bit one. In the 32-bit version, MongoDB has the limitation of storage size, that is, you cannot store datasets more than 2 GB.

While using a 32-bit version, if the database storage is more than 2 GB, you will get an error, and you can't start the server till the time you remove your data or migrate your database to a 64-bit version of MongoDB.

The Unix limitation

Most of the Unix family systems such as OS X and Linux provide a method to limit the amount of resources that each user and process can use at the moment. The `ulimit` function is responsible for managing and applying this limitation.

When the mongod or mongos processes reach the limitation, some errors will show up and the MongoDB server will crash at that moment. You can simply change the limitation using the ulimit function.

Both mongod and mongos instances need to connect to other nodes, members and clients, so it's recommended that you change the limitation manually to prevent problems in the production and for high throughput.

By using the ulimit -a command, you can see the limitations. The following screenshot is an example of using this command:

```
➜  ~  ulimit -a
-t: cpu time (seconds)               unlimited
-f: file size (blocks)               unlimited
-d: data seg size (kbytes)           unlimited
-s: stack size (kbytes)              8192
-c: core file size (blocks)          0
-v: address space (kbytes)           unlimited
-l: locked-in-memory size (kbytes)   unlimited
-u: processes                        709
-n: file descriptors                 256
```

The ulimit command shows you the limitation per user. So, if you run the mongod or mongos instances as a user, you will realize that these processes might reach this limitation.

 Note that the processes' value (that is, -u) refers to the combined number of distinct processes and subprocess threads. This can be accessed at http://docs.mongodb.org/manual/reference/ulimit/.

To change the limitation, you can simply use the following command:

```
ulimit -a 256
```

After changing the limitation, its better to restart the mongod or mongos instances to apply the limitation.

The following is the recommended setting for the mongod and mongos processes from the MongoDB documentation page at http://docs.mongodb.org/manual/reference/ulimit/. The settings are set using the following command:

```
-f (file size): unlimited
-t (cpu time): unlimited
```

```
-v (virtual memory): unlimited

-n (open files): 64000

-m (memory size): unlimited

-u (processes/threads): 32000
```

Failover in replica set

In MongoDB, we have a feature that enables clustering for a database. This feature is called a replica set. In further chapters, we will introduce and review it in detail. However, for this chapter, a brief introduction to this feature is enough.

 A replica set in MongoDB is a group of mongod processes that maintain the same dataset. Replica sets provide redundancy and high availability and are the basis for all production deployments. For more information, please visit http://docs.mongodb.org/manual/replication/.

In replica sets, when the primary node becomes unavailable, the replica set conducts an election process to choose a new primary member from secondaries. This change might take about 10 to 60 seconds. However, it varies between servers and depends on the replica set settings, numbers of nodes, and server capacity.

While performing the election process, the replica set becomes unavailable for write operations. So, in this situation, operations are limited and you cannot perform write operations until the primary node is available.

There are several ways to address these kinds of issues, such as providing an internal loop statement and trying to insert data until the primary node becomes available. On the other hand, using a queue system and putting all the write operations in it and then applying them when the primary node becomes available is another solution.

In further chapters, we will talk about the high availability of replica sets in detail.

Sharding the configuration server failure

To distribute the whole dataset to different machines and servers, that is, horizontal scaling, MongoDB provides you with the sharding feature. Using this feature, you can split the database into different pieces in separate servers. In the next chapters, we will learn more about this feature in detail.

MongoDB uses configuration servers to store the configuration for the sharding settings and relations between members. For the production environment, these configuration servers are exactly three in number.

If one or two distinct configuration servers become unavailable, the clustering works properly, but it cannot create more chunks from the dataset, which means that it will be read-only.

Chunks are pieces of database in separate machines, and MongoDB splits the database into chunks of data based on a sharded key. MongoDB creates chunks from the database after write operations based on the given sharded key.

If all three configuration servers become unavailable, the cluster will be unavailable as well. You should replace the configuration servers as soon as possible. Then, the cluster will continue to use the configuration servers and work properly.

We will talk about sharded keys and chunks in detail in the next chapters.

Understanding database locks

MongoDB uses read/write locks to prevent conflicts between write/read operations and also makes sure that all clients receive the same dataset with the same query.

MongoDB uses the readers-writer lock to prevent conflicts and control the read/write operations.

 A readers-writer lock is like a mutex, in that, it controls access to a shared resource, allowing concurrent access to multiple threads for reading, but restricting access to a single thread for writes (or other changes) to the resource. For more information, please visit http://en.wikipedia.org/wiki/Readers%E2%80%93writer_lock.

MongoDB uses the shared read-lock, which means that many operations can use the existing read-lock. On the other hand, a write-lock is limited to a single operation, which means that no more write operations can use and share the existing lock.

The MongoDB lock mechanism gets better with each version. Before v2.2, MongoDB had a global lock per mongod instance for most read/write operations. This means that the lock is shared between all databases on a MongoDB instance and a lock on a database blocks operations for all other databases.

After v2.2, this limitation changed and the lock was limited to a database and not all databases of a `mongod` instance. For instance, if you have three databases in a single instance and one database creates a lock, then the other two databases become available for write/read operations.

Furthermore, MongoDB locks are "writer greedy", which means that if both read/write operations are waiting for a lock, the write operation gets more priority, and MongoDB gives the lock to the write operation first.

 You can read more about concurrency and read/write locks at `http://docs.mongodb.org/manual/faq/concurrency/`.

Summary

In this chapter, you learned the basic reasons for MongoDB failures and the situations in which they might happen. We learned that the 32-bit version of MongoDB has some issues in the production environment, and it's necessary to use a 64-bit version for production only to prevent issues in high load.

After this, we learned about the `ulimit` function in Unix family operating systems, which enable us to manage limitations for processes or change the limitation easily via the command-line environment. Most of the time, MongoDB can reach this limitation and crashes due to not having enough resources.

We then went on to discover that while replica sets are available for failover and the election process, MongoDB is not available for write operations. Hence, we need to provide a way to control the write operations and prevent data loss.

Then, we saw that the unavailability of configuration servers can cause issues for the sharded cluster, and at least one configuration server should be available for the cluster. Next, we reviewed the lock types of MongoDB for read/write operations, which prevents operation conflicts and ensures that all clients receive the same view from the database.

In the next chapter, we will learn about the basic concepts of MongoDB clustering and how we can create a cluster network in MongoDB to provide a readily available server.

Clustering in MongoDB 3

As a database gets larger, you need to come up with solutions to improve its performance to support more queries over a period of time and throughput. The most common solution in databases is clustering. Using clustering, you can save data across multiple servers and obviously, share and distribute the pressure of data between different servers. In this chapter, you will learn the basic concepts of clustering in MongoDB.

Sharding in MongoDB

MongoDB has a great solution to provide clustering. **Sharding** is one of the remarkable MongoDB features that enable developers to easily create a cluster in MongoDB using different `mongod` instances in between the servers.

Sharding consists of various parts such as replica sets and configuration servers. Before discussing more about clustering and sharding, you need to learn the basic terms of clustering in MongoDB. In the next sections, we will discuss different aspects of the sharding architecture.

Understanding replication

To start with, you need to know the basic components of sharding in MongoDB. One of the major features required for clustering in MongoDB is **replication**. Replication is a procedure to synchronize data through various servers. Actually, by using replication, you can save or copy the same data between different servers, so this redundancy can protect the database from the data loss of a single server.

Furthermore, replication allows you to use other servers as a backup or reporting server. In some clients, you can send read operations to another server, which results in an increase in read capacity and performance.

Learning about a replica set

The **replica set** is a collection of mongod processes. Each replica set has one and only one primary mongod process that accepts all write and read operations from the clients. All other mongod processes are known as secondaries; they copy all operations from the primary node and apply them so that all secondaries have the same data at once, along with the replication log at varying speeds. This lag depends on the amount of data, network speed, and so on.

The data synchronization procedure happens with the help of replication. To support replication, the primary node will record all write operations in its oplog.

The following diagram illustrates the relations between clients, primary, and secondary nodes:

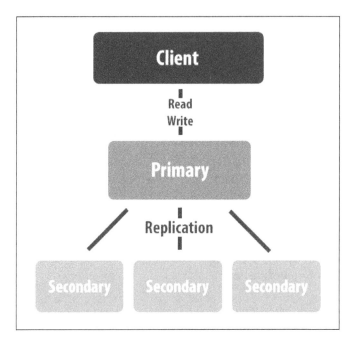

What is oplog?

The `oplog` is a capped collection (a fixed-sized collection) of data that keeps a record of all data altering operations. The `primary` node will update the dataset and modify its `oplog`, and then secondaries will copy `oplog` from the `primary` node and apply the operations in an asynchronous procedure.

To read more about `oplog` and its operation, you can visit `http://docs.mongodb.org/manual/core/replica-set-oplog/`.

`Secondary` nodes will download and apply primary's `oplog`, that is, secondaries that have the same dataset. As already mentioned, each replica set has one and only one `primary` node that accepts all read/write operations. If the `primary` node is unavailable, another `secondary` node will be the `primary` node that uses an election process. A `secondary` node will be elected to a `primary` node if there is a clear majority vote for a node.

By default, clients read from the `primary` node; however, clients can specify a read preference to send read operations to secondaries at `http://docs.mongodb.org/manual/core/replication-introduction/`.

To update the nodes' availability, each node sends a ping or heartbeat packets to all other nodes. The following diagram illustrates this process:

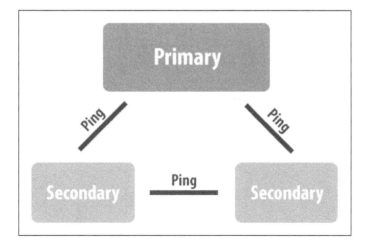

To facilitate the election process, you can add an extra mongod node as an arbiter node. Arbiter nodes don't have any dataset. Arbiter nodes exist to vote in the election process. They come in handy when you have an even number of nodes, so these nodes can help you to choose the correct secondary node for the primary node.

What is an arbiter?

Arbiter is a mongod node that doesn't have any dataset and can't become a primary node. Arbiter nodes exist to vote in the election process of a primary node. They don't need dedicated hardware.

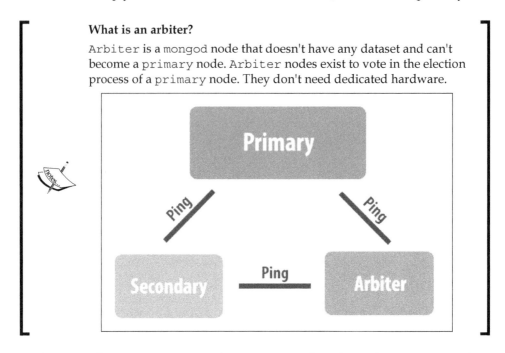

Secondaries apply oplog in an asynchronous procedure from the primary node.

When the primary node of a replica set doesn't send or receive a ping (heartbeat) message for 10 seconds with other nodes, the replica set will conduct an election to choose the primary node from secondaries. The secondary node that has the majority of votes becomes the primary node. Of course, the arbiter node comes in handy in this situation.

When the old primary node comes online again, it will become a new secondary node.

The following chart shows you the procedure of the election process and the procedure of choosing a new `primary` node:

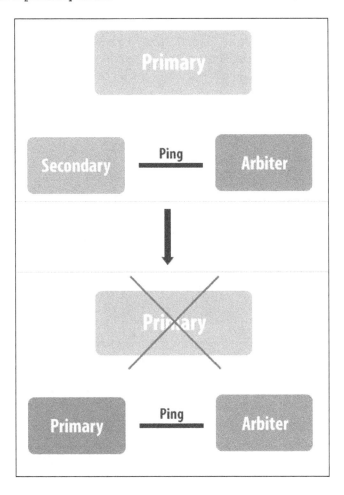

Vertical and horizontal scaling

The database systems can be scaled with two basic approaches, vertical or horizontal. In the vertical scaling approach, you need to add more capacity to the existing server, for instance, adding more CPU, RAM or storage to the server. It's obvious that adding more CPU or RAM to the existing server is more expensive and difficult to maintain. The following diagram shows you the process of vertical scaling:

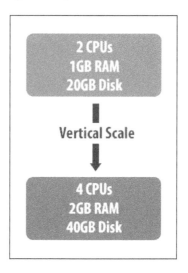

In horizontal scaling, the database system can be scaled through different servers instead of only one server, that is, the database is scaled horizontally rather than vertically. This approach is safer, easier, and less expensive than vertical scaling. The process of horizontal scaling is shown in the following diagram:

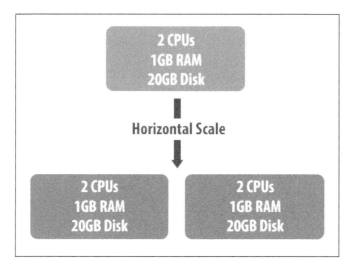

Utilizing sharding

Sharding is the solution to address scaling issues in MongoDB. Using sharding, developers can horizontally scale the database over multiple servers. The same dataset is divided over multiple servers. Each individual server calls the shard; it is an independent database. All shards together make the single logical database.

The following diagram shows you the sharding process:

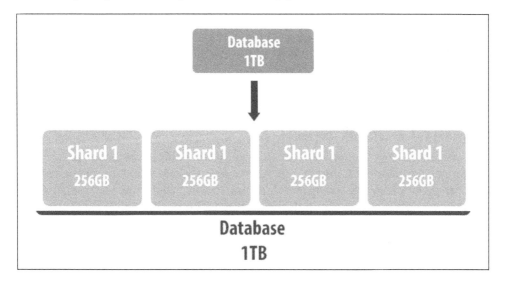

Sharding solves the problem of high overload and large datasets. While inserting or reading data, the client or application needs to access only one shard and not all shards. Hence, this change will horizontally scale the throughput and overload. Consequently, the database can support more operations.

On the other hand, by dividing the whole database over different servers, it reduces the amount of data that each server should store. Hence, each shard holds only a specific part of the whole database. As a result, to store 1 TB database using sharding, you can have four different servers, each having a storage of 256 GB. By adding more shards, you can reduce the storage size of each server.

Implementing clustering in MongoDB

In this section, we will go through the implementation of a cluster in MongoDB using sharding and replica sets.

 A sharded cluster consists of three configuration processes, one or more replica sets, and one or more mongos routing processes.

You can view this at http://docs.mongodb.org/manual/reference/glossary/#term-sharded-cluster.

A sharded cluster in MongoDB consists of three components, configuration servers, shards (replica sets or mongod processes), and mongos. The mongos process is the query router for all clients.

Learning about shards

Shards are replica sets that store each individual part of a database. In a development environment, you can use the mongod process instead of the replica set, but for production, it's recommended that you use the replica set because it provides better performance in high throughput. The replica set is made up of different mongod processes.

Understanding the configuration server

Configuration servers are used to store the cluster network and each node's metadata. For instance, configuration servers store the mapping dataset in each shard. In the production environment, it's recommended that you use exactly three configuration servers.

Utilizing the mongos or query router

The query router or mongos process is the interface for client and applications, that is, the application will send the request to the mongos process, and it will route the request to the corresponding shard. After completing the operation, mongos will send the result to the client. The point of having query routers in sharded clusters is to divide the load between different mongod processes. A sharded cluster can have one or more query routers, and for a production deployment, it would be better to have more than one query router.

The following diagram shows you the relationship between different components of a sharded cluster in a production environment:

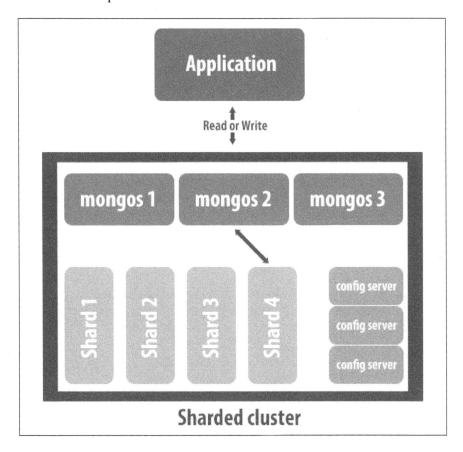

A sharded cluster uses a shard key to distribute the dataset through shards, or it divides the database. There are two different approaches to choose a shard key: range-based partitioning and hash-based partitioning. In the coming chapters, you will learn about these two approaches in detail.

Summary

This chapter was more practical than previous chapters, because you learned the basics of creating and developing a cluster network in MongoDB in order to make a MongoDB server.

First of all, you learned about the replication procedure and how it works. Then, you had a brief description of the replica set architecture. Next, we talked about the replica set failover, how it works, and the replica set election process. We also gave you a detailed explanation of replica set members such as the `primary`, `secondary`, and `arbiter` nodes.

Next, you learned about the sharding network in MongoDB that gives developers the ability to make a sharded cluster network and divide the database over different servers. This action helps us make the MongoDB server mush faster and easier to manage. Furthermore, we learned about vertical and horizontal scaling and why horizontal scaling is better and more efficient than vertical scaling. We also learned about sharded cluster network members such as the configuration server, shards, and query routers.

In the next chapter, we will talk in detail about creating a sharded cluster and replica set network in a real-world example. Furthermore, we will learn how to choose a sharded key for different purposes based on our data.

4
Utilizing a Replica Set

In this chapter, we will discuss replication and the replica set in detail, along with some examples. We will learn about the basic configuration and architectures required to establish a replica set network and also how the replication procedure works in a replica set.

Besides this, you will learn the purpose of replication and a replica set, deployment patterns of replica sets, and details about replica set's members and failover processes.

The purpose of replication

There are some terms in MongoDB that are used together. Replica set and replication procedures are two terms that work together to provide a readily available MongoDB server.

Understanding replication

Replication is the process of synchronizing data across multiple servers. (http://docs.mongodb.org/manual/core/replication-introduction/).

In a replica set, each node can be hosted in different servers. Hence, you need to synchronize data between all nodes. MongoDB named this procedure **replication**. The following diagram shows you the process of replication:

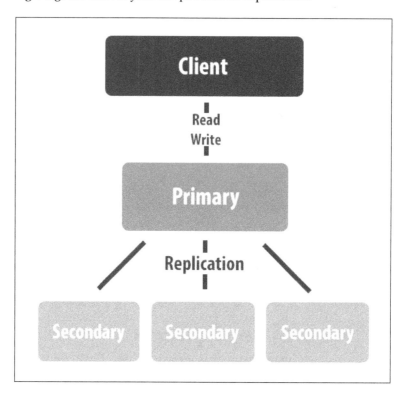

You can see the replication procedure in the preceding diagram that is used to synchronize data between the primary node, which accepts all read/write operations, and secondary nodes. Thus, all secondary nodes and primary nodes will have the same dataset after completing the synchronization process.

With the replication procedure, you will have redundancy in your database, but this redundancy brings data availability. Furthermore, multiple copies of a single database protect the database from failure, data loss, or hardware crashes. On the other hand, you can simply assign a dedicated server for backup or failure recovery. Actually, each server contains an individual MongoDB instance.

Additionally, MongoDB clients can send the read operations to different servers; consequently, using this approach, you can increase the read performance in high load.

Understanding asynchronous replication

The whole replication process can be asynchronous, that is, the `secondary` nodes perform replication in an asynchronous process. As the synchronization process takes time, some `secondary` nodes might not have the exact dataset as `primary`.

Architecture of replica sets

After learning the replication process, we can go ahead and learn about the replica set architecture. In order to create a readily available MongoDB server, you can simply use the replica set network.

So, what is replica set?

A replica set is a group of `mongod` instances that host the same dataset (http://docs.mongodb.org/manual/core/replication-introduction/).

Each replica set consists of different members and each one is responsible for a particular task. The following list shows you all the possible roles for each member:

- `Primary`: A `primary` node is responsible for accepting all read/write operations from clients. Each replica set can have one and only one `primary` node. Under some conditions, a `primary` node can become `secondary` or a `secondary` node can become `primary` by an election process.

- `Secondary`: The `secondary` nodes host the same dataset as `primary` nodes. Each replica set can have one or more `secondary` nodes. It's possible that a `secondary` node changes its state and becomes a `primary` node by the election process.

- `Arbiter`: An `arbiter` node is used to facilitate the election procedure. An `arbiter` node won't change its state. The `arbiter` node doesn't host any dataset and only votes in the election process. On the other hand, the `arbiter` node doesn't need any dedicated hardware.

The following screenshot illustrates the architecture of `primary`, `secondary`, and `arbiter` nodes:

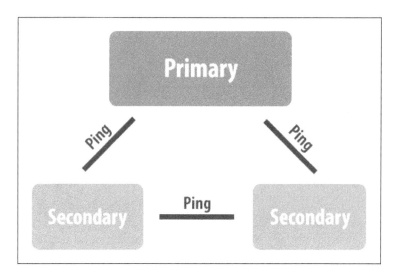

Each replica set can have up to 12 members, out of which 7 can vote in an election. If you need more than 12 members for production, you should use the master-slave replication, which is not recommended by MongoDB because it lacks in the failover process.

Read more about master-slave replication at `http://docs.mongodb.org/manual/core/master-slave/`.

Understanding oplog

`Oplog` is used to record all database changes in a collection of data.

An `oplog` (operations log) is a special capped collection that keeps a rolling record of all the operations that modify the data stored in your databases (`http://docs.mongodb.org/manual/core/replica-set-oplog/`).

It is a fixed-size collection, and it will automatically overwrite old records when it reaches the maximum size of the collection. `Oplog` is used in the replication procedure to facilitate the process of replication between `primary` and `secondary` nodes.

The `secondary` nodes copy the primary's `oplog` and apply it, so all members will have `oplog` that saves the current state and recent history of the database.

The first time you add a replica set to the database, the server creates `oplog` with its default size. The size of `oplog` varies, and it depends on the operating system and machine architecture. However, you can define and change the default size of `oplog` using the `oplogSize` property.

The following list shows you the default values for the `oplog` size based on different operating systems:

- For 64-bit Linux, Solaris, FreeBSD, and Windows systems, MongoDB allocates 5 percent of the available free disk space to `oplog`. If this amount is smaller than a gigabyte, then MongoDB allocates 1 gigabyte of space.

- For 64-bit OS X systems, MongoDB allocates 183 megabytes of space to `oplog`.

- For 32-bit systems, MongoDB allocates about 48 megabytes of space to `oplog` (`http://docs.mongodb.org/manual/core/replica-set-oplog/`).

To check the status of `oplog` and monitor the size of the log and collection, you can use the following command and run it in the MongoDB shell:

```
db.printReplicationInfo()
```

Learning about replication and oplog changes

Clients send write operations to the `primary` node, and it applies the operation and writes it to its `oplog`. The secondary members will copy and apply primary's `oplog` in order to duplicate the primary's dataset. This procedure happens in an asynchronous replication.

Clients can't send the write operation to `secondary` nodes, but they can send read operations to secondaries. By default, all clients send both read/write operations to the `primary` node. However, modifying the configurations can change this.

Understanding nodes' failover

In order to get information about each node's availability, nodes direct ping messages to each other to show their availability, as illustrated in the following diagram:

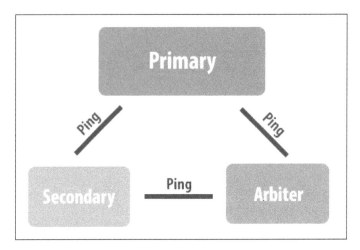

In some situations, the primary node might become unavailable. If the primary node doesn't communicate with other members for more than 10 seconds, the replica set will conduct an election to choose a new primary node from the secondary members.

Understanding the replica set election process

The secondary node with the majority of votes becomes a primary node. If the previous primary node becomes available again, it will become a secondary node.

The following diagram demonstrates a replica set with a primary and secondary member and one arbiter node:

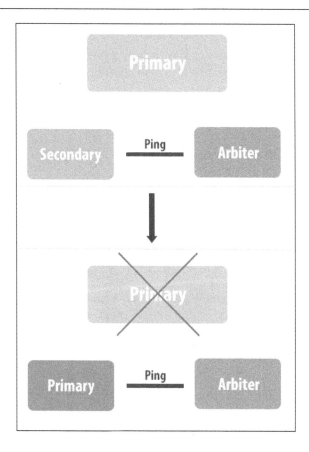

In the preceding replica set, because we have only one `secondary` and an `arbiter` node, if the `primary` node becomes unavailable; the `arbiter` node votes for the only `secondary` node available, and the replica set will choose the only secondary member as the primary. However, the `arbiter` node won't change its state.

Different forms of secondary members

The secondary members can be defined for various purposes by changing the default member's configuration. A secondary member can be configured to the following:

- The priority 0 member.
- The hidden member.
- The delayed member.
- To design an efficient replica set, each type of member becomes handy in some cases. In next parts of the chapter, you can read the purpose of each kind of the aforementioned secondary members.

Using the priority 0 member

Although these kinds of members cannot become primary, they function as normal secondary members. This means that the priority 0 members contains the same dataset as a `primary` node, accepts read operations, and also votes in the election process.

 Members have priority equal to 1 by default.

The following diagram shows you a replica set with three members: one `primary` node, and two `secondary` nodes. The first `secondary` node (the green box) can become `primary`, but the second `secondary` node (the gray box) can't change its state because it's a priority 0 member. This is shown in the following diagram:

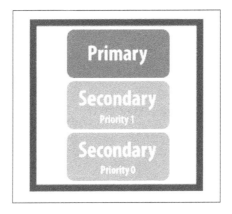

Also, a priority 0 member can be hosted in a dedicated machine. The following diagram illustrates this case:

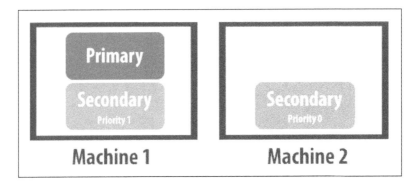

Like the previous example, the `secondary` node in **Machine 2** cannot become `primary` because the configuration of this node defines it as a priority 0 member.

The following is a sample configuration for a priority 0 member:

```
{
  "_id" : <num>,
  "host" : <hostname:port>,
  "priority" : 0
}
```

Utilizing hidden members

The hidden members are a subset of priority 0 members because they have priority that is equal to 0. These kind of members hold the same dataset as primary, but this will be invisible to all the clients. Accordingly, hidden members won't receive any read/write operations, and as a result, they won't receive any traffic except normal replication and the syncing process between `primary` node. In contrast, hidden members can vote in an election.

Because hidden members will not receive any traffic, the main usage of the hidden member can be for dedicated tasks such as reporting, backup, or disaster recovery server. The following diagram shows you how to utilize hidden members:

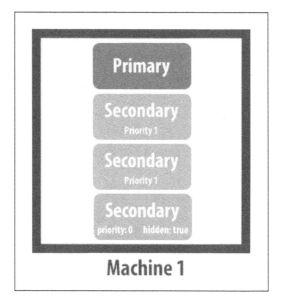

The preceding diagram shows you a replica set with four members: the primary member, two `secondary` nodes with priority 1, and a `secondary` node that is hidden with primary 0.

The last secondary member will be hidden from clients, and they can't route their read operations to this node.

The delayed member

The delayed secondary member is a hidden and obviously a priority 0 member. Actually, it is a subset of hidden members.

A delayed member's dataset is the same as the `primary` node but with a specified delay. For instance, if the member syncs itself with a `primary` node now, if the current time is 10:00 A.M., and the member has a delay of one hour (or 3600 seconds), this member will sync the dataset with the `primary` node again will be at 11:00 A.M. In other words, a delayed member copies and applies `oplog` with a specific delay.

This behavior comes in handy when you want to keep an older version of the dataset to prevent human errors, software upgrade issues, or invalid data entries.

However, a delayed member can vote in an election process, as shown in the following diagram:

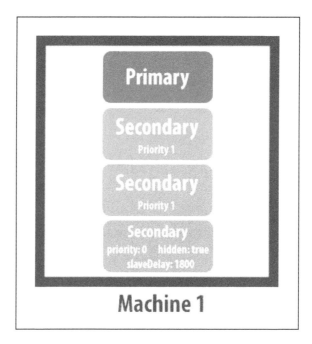

The preceding diagram illustrates a replica set that consists of four members: a primary, two secondary members with priority 1, both of which can become primary, and a delayed secondary node with a delay of 1800 seconds or half an hour.

The following is a sample configuration for a delayed member:

```
{
    "_id" : <num>,
    "host" : <hostname:port>,
    "priority" : 0,
    "slaveDelay" : <seconds>,
    "hidden" : true
}
```

Understanding the arbiter node's role

An `arbiter` node doesn't have any dataset, hence it doesn't accept read/write operations. The arbiter member votes in the replica set election process for a `secondary` node to become `primary`. An `arbiter` node comes useful when you have an even number of replica set members or not enough servers for a new member.

 Add an `arbiter` node to a replica set only when there is an even number of members. If you add an `arbiter` node to a set with an odd number of members, the set might suffer from tied elections. For more information, you can visit `http://docs.mongodb.org/manual/core/replica-set-arbiter/`.

The following diagram shows you a replica set with an even number of members:

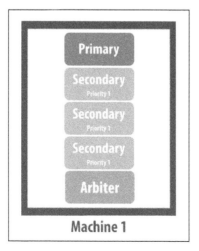

The preceding diagram enables a replica set to have an odd number of votes and prevent the replica set from the tied election problem.

Summary

In this chapter, you learned the basic configuration and concepts of the replication process and the replica set network. We talked about the basic type of members, including the primary, secondary, and arbiter members. Then, we learned about the `oplog` collection, which holds the database changes.

Then, we went through the different kinds of secondary members. Primary 0, hidden, and delayed members are different types of secondary members. Also, you can find a detailed description explaining each one with illustrated charts and diagrams.

Moreover, you learned about the `arbiter` nodes that don't store any data but vote in the election process for a new primary member.

In the next chapter, we will deploy a replica set network from scratch to provide a readily available MongoDB server.

5
Replica Set in Action

In the previous chapters, you learned the basic terms and fundamentals needed to work with a replica set network in MongoDB. Now, it's time to examine a replica set in action through a practical example.

In this chapter, we will set up a new replica set from scratch to provide a readily available MongoDB server. Furthermore, we will see the failover process of replica sets in action. You will learn all the steps using screenshots, so it will be easier to follow the procedure.

Overview of replica sets

There are two ways to deploy a replica set, for production or development, and testing. In this chapter, we will deploy replica set for production use. The same procedure is used to deploy a replica set in a development environment, but the requirements are different.

A three-member replica set can provide enough power to overcome network and server issues. To have a smooth election process, it's recommended that you have an odd number of members in a replica set.

The following diagram shows a replica set with three members:

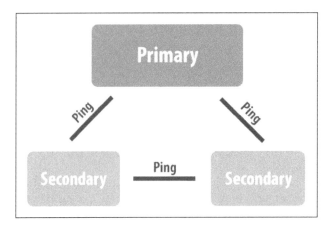

Likewise, for production use of a replica set, each replica set should be hosted on different machines. As you are aware, each machine can face network or hardware failure, so by hosting Missing object type instance on different machines, we can make sure that if a machine fails, we won't lose all the mongod processes.

Before deploying a replica set

There are some steps you need to take before starting a replica set deployment. First of all, you should make sure that you have the latest stable version of MongoDB on each machine.

 If you haven't installed MongoDB yet and need help installing MongoDB, read these short instructions at http://docs.mongodb. org/manual/installation/.

Additionally, before deploying a replica set, you must make sure that there aren't any network issues between replica set members. Each machine must see the other, and you must configure the firewall not to prevent connections. In order to have an effective replica set, you should configure the machine so that every member can connect to the other.

 If you want a procedure to check the connection between members, visit http://docs.mongodb.org/manual/tutorial/troubleshoot-replica-sets/#replica-set-troubleshooting-check-connection.

Configurations of a replica set

In our example, we will create a replica set using three members on different machines. The following is the configuration of each machine:

- Mac OS X 10.9.2
- Ubuntu 12.04
- Ubuntu 12.04

We have Mac OS X on our host machine, and we use VMware Fusion to run other machines at once. The network connections between members are provided by VMware Fusion. Each `mongod` object will be hosted on different machines, so we will have three members on three separate machines.

The following scheme shows each machine's hostname:

- `mongod1.replicaset.com`
- `mongod2.replicaset.com`
- `mongod3.replicaset.com`

You can set up hostnames by configuring DNS settings or adding hostnames to the `hosts` file. This file can be found in the `/etc/` folder of the Unix operating systems.

The following diagram shows the member's network and relationships:

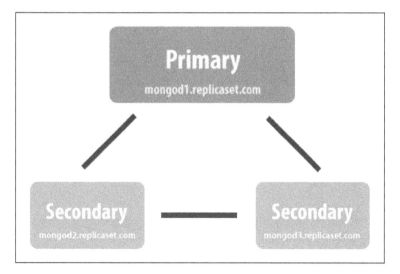

It's obvious that according to the situation, secondaries can become primaries. For instance, if mongod2.replicaset.com receives the majority of the votes, it will become the primary in place of mongod1.replicaset.com.

The next step will be preparing the configuration file. There are two ways to define the configuration for MongoDB via a shell or by creating a configuration file. To run mongod in a production environment, you must define the configurations in a file and set the filepath to mongod in shell. To start mongod or mongos with a configuration file, the following commands can be used:

```
mongod --config /etc/mongodb.conf
mongod -f /etc/mongodb.conf
mongos --config /srv/mongodb/mongos.conf
mongos -f /srv/mongodb/mongos.conf
```

In this example, we use the /etc/mongodb.conf path to store the configuration file. The following configuration shows our file content:

```
dbpath = /usr/local/var/mongodb
logpath = /var/log/mongodb.log
bind_ip = 127.0.0.1
port = 27017
fork = true
replSet = rs1
```

We will review some of the important options briefly. In order to define the path of the stored data, you should use the dbpath property. Also, the logpath property defines the path of the logfile. Using the bind_ip command, you can define the network interface that mongod or mongos will listen to. Without defining this property, MongoDB accepts all connections from all network interfaces. Consequently, you need to configure the firewall properly to prevent unexpected connections.

The port property defines the port number; the process will listen on this port. It would be better to leave this property and use the mongod default port, but for educational purposes we will use it and set the port to the mongod default port number, which is 27017.

Additionally, using the fork property, you can run mongod or mongos as a daemon. To use this property, you must already define the logpath in the configuration.

The last property is replSet, which is used to define the replica set name.

For more information on properties and options, you can read the documentation at `http://docs.mongodb.org/manual/reference/configuration-options/`.

After saving the config file, you can run the `mongod` instances using the `--config` parameter.

The following screenshot illustrates the result of executing the `mongod` command with the `--config` parameter:

```
➜  ~   sudo mongod --config /etc/mongodb.conf
forked process: 82674
all output going to: /var/log/mongodb.log
```

Deploying a replica set

Having completed the initialization steps, we can now start to define our first replica set. First of all, you need to run the `mongod` process on all machines through the following steps:

1. Make sure that you have the configuration file in your machine, and then run the following command:

   ```
   mongod --config /etc/mongodb.conf
   ```

    In Unix operating systems, if you don't have sufficient permissions to run the command, you can use the `sudo` prefix. So the complete command will be `sudo mongod --config /etc/mongodb.conf`.

2. After issuing the command, you should see the result depicted in the following screenshot:

   ```
   ➜  ~   sudo mongod --config /etc/mongodb.conf
   forked process: 82772
   all output going to: /var/log/mongodb.log
   ```

3. Because we set the fork property to true, `mongod` will run as a daemon in the background. So, in order to see the logs and outputs of `mongod`, you should use the defined `logpath` file. You can see the logfile content as shown in the following screenshot:

```
→ ~  cat /var/log/mongodb.log
Thu Apr 10 17:58:51 [initandlisten] MongoDB starting : pid=82855 port=27017 dbpath=/usr/local/var/mongodb 64-bit host
=mongod1.replicaset.com
Thu Apr 10 17:58:51 [initandlisten] db version v2.0.0, pdfile version 4.5
Thu Apr 10 17:58:51 [initandlisten] git version: 695c67dff0ffc361b8568a13366f027caa406222
Thu Apr 10 17:58:51 [initandlisten] build info: Darwin erh2.10gen.cc 9.6.0 Darwin Kernel Version 9.6.0: Mon Nov 24 17
:37:00 PST 2008; root:xnu-1228.9.59~1/RELEASE_I386 i386 BOOST_LIB_VERSION=1_40
Thu Apr 10 17:58:51 [initandlisten] options: { bind_ip: "127.0.0.1", config: "/etc/mongodb.conf", dbpath: "/usr/local
/var/mongodb", fork: "true", logpath: "/var/log/mongodb.log", port: 27017, replSet: "rs1" }
Thu Apr 10 17:58:51 [initandlisten] journal dir=/usr/local/var/mongodb/journal
Thu Apr 10 17:58:51 [initandlisten] recover : no journal files present, no recovery needed
Thu Apr 10 17:58:51 [websvr] admin web console waiting for connections on port 28017
Thu Apr 10 17:58:51 [initandlisten] waiting for connections on port 27017
Thu Apr 10 17:58:51 [initandlisten] connection accepted from 127.0.0.1:61874 #1
Thu Apr 10 17:58:51 [rsStart] replSet can't get local.system.replset config from self or any seed (EMPTYCONFIG)
Thu Apr 10 17:58:51 [rsStart] replSet info you may need to run replSetInitiate -- rs.initiate() in the shell -- if th
at is not already done
```

4. For the next steps, you should use `mongo` interactive shell to run and configure the replica set.

5. Run the `mongo` command from your command environment and you will get the following screenshot:

```
→ /etc  mongo
MongoDB shell version: 2.6.0
connecting to: test
```

6. Then, run the following command in `mongo` to initiate the replica set:

    `rs.initiate()`

7. After executing the preceding command, you should see a result similar to the one depicted in the following screenshot:

```
> rs.initiate()
{
        "info2" : "no configuration explicitly specified -- making one",
        "me" : "mongod1.replicaset.com:27017",
        "info" : "Config now saved locally.  Should come online in about a minute.",
        "ok" : 1
}
```

If the initialization of the replica set is successful, you will see the `ok: 1` message from the `mongo` process.

Using the rs.conf() command in mongo, you can get the replica set configuration. The following screenshot shows the output of this command:

```
PRIMARY> rs.conf()
{
        "_id" : "rs1",
        "version" : 1,
        "members" : [
                {
                        "_id" : 0,
                        "host" : "mongod1.replicaset.com:27017"
                }
        ]
}
```

As you can see, the _id property shows the name of our replica set, and we currently have only one member, the primary node.

Also, you can see the address and port of each member in the host property. Our primary node's host is mongod1.replicaset.com, and the port number is 27017.

In the next section, you will learn how to add other members to our replica set and manage other nodes from the mongo shell.

Adding a new member

After creating the master node or the primary node, you can add other members, including secondaries and arbiters to it.

So far, we have configured mongod1.replicaset.com, and now we should add mongod2.replicaset.com and mongo3.replicaset.com to the primary machine. This process is listed in the following steps:

1. Adding a new member to an existing replica set is as easy as calling the following command in the mongo shell:

    ```
    rs.add("mongod2.replicaset.com")
    ```

2. Before running the preceding command in the first machine, you should make sure that you have already copied the MongoDB configuration file. It's recommended that you stop the current running mongod, copy the configuration file to the target machine (or make it again), and then start mongod using the --config parameter again.

3. After issuing the preceding command, you should see the result in the `mongo` shell as shown in the following screenshot:

```
PRIMARY> rs.add("mongod2.replicaset.com")
{ "ok" : 1 }
```

4. You can simply execute the `rs.status()` command to see the whole replica set status each time. The following screenshot shows the status of our replica set network at this step:

```
PRIMARY> rs.status()
{
        "set" : "rs1",
        "date" : ISODate("2014-04-11T15:58:21Z"),
        "myState" : 1,
        "members" : [
                {
                        "_id" : 0,
                        "name" : "mongod1.replicaset.com:27017",
                        "health" : 1,
                        "state" : 1,
                        "stateStr" : "PRIMARY",
                        "optime" : {
                                "t" : 1397231359000,
                                "i" : 1
                        },
                        "optimeDate" : ISODate("2014-04-11T15:49:19Z"),
                        "self" : true
                },
                {
                        "_id" : 1,
                        "name" : "mongod2.replicaset.com:27017",
                        "health" : 1,
                        "state" : 5,
                        "stateStr" : "STARTUP2",
                        "uptime" : 22,
                        "optime" : {
                                "t" : 0,
                                "i" : 0
                        },
                        "optimeDate" : ISODate("1970-01-01T00:00:00Z"),
                        "lastHeartbeat" : ISODate("2014-04-11T15:58:19Z"),
                        "pingMs" : 0,
                        "errmsg" : "initial sync need a member to be primary or secondary to do our initial sync"
                }
        ],
        "ok" : 1
}
```

5. For the next step of configuring the replica set, you should add the third member. Our member's hostname is `mongod3.replicaset.com`. Again, you can add the member using the `rs.add()` method as shown in the following screenshot:

```
PRIMARY> rs.add("mongod3.replicaset.com")
{ "ok" : 1 }
```

6. After adding the third member, we have a three-member replica set. Again, by issuing the `rs.status()` command in the `mongo` shell, you can check the status of the replica set. The following screenshot illustrates the status of our replica set network after adding the third member to it:

```
{
        "set" : "rs1",
        "date" : ISODate("2014-04-11T15:58:44Z"),
        "myState" : 1,
        "members" : [
                {
                        "_id" : 0,
                        "name" : "mongod1.replicaset.com:27017",
                        "health" : 1,
                        "state" : 1,
                        "stateStr" : "PRIMARY",
                        "optime" : {
                                "t" : 1397231918000,
                                "i" : 1
                        },
                        "optimeDate" : ISODate("2014-04-11T15:58:38Z"),
                        "self" : true
                },
                {
                        "_id" : 1,
                        "name" : "mongod2.replicaset.com:27017",
                        "health" : 1,
                        "state" : 2,
                        "stateStr" : "SECONDARY",
                        "uptime" : 45,
                        "optime" : {
                                "t" : 1397231918000,
                                "i" : 1
                        },
                        "optimeDate" : ISODate("2014-04-11T15:58:38Z"),
                        "lastHeartbeat" : ISODate("2014-04-11T15:58:43Z"),
                        "pingMs" : 0
                },
                {
                        "_id" : 2,
                        "name" : "mongod3.replicaset.com:27017",
                        "health" : 1,
                        "state" : 6,
                        "stateStr" : "UNKNOWN",
                        "uptime" : 6,
                        "optime" : {
                                "t" : 0,
                                "i" : 0
                        },
                        "optimeDate" : ISODate("1970-01-01T00:00:00Z"),
                        "lastHeartbeat" : ISODate("2014-04-11T15:58:42Z"),
                        "pingMs" : 0,
                        "errmsg" : "still initializing"
                }
        ],
        "ok" : 1
}
```

7. As you can see in the preceding screenshot, after a while, mongod2. replicaset.com becomes primary. In the secondary machine's mongo shell, you can see the result shown in the following screenshot:

```
rs1:RECOVERING>
rs1:SECONDARY>
```

8. The mongod object goes to the recovering mode, and after a while, you can see the status of the secondary node becomes secondary. The reason for using the recovering mode at first is to sync the data with the primary node.

 Usually, syncing takes less than a minute for an empty dataset, but if you're running the replica set on an existing dbpath object, it depends on the size of oplog.

9. After syncing data between primary and secondary nodes, you can see the following status page from the primary node:

```
PRIMARY> rs.status()
{
    "set" : "rs1",
    "date" : ISODate("2014-04-11T15:59:26Z"),
    "myState" : 1,
    "members" : [
        {
            "_id" : 0,
            "name" : "mongod1.replicaset.com:27017",
            "health" : 1,
            "state" : 1,
            "stateStr" : "PRIMARY",
            "optime" : {
                "t" : 1397231918000,
                "i" : 1
            },
            "optimeDate" : ISODate("2014-04-11T15:58:38Z"),
            "self" : true
        },
        {
            "_id" : 1,
            "name" : "mongod2.replicaset.com:27017",
            "health" : 1,
            "state" : 2,
            "stateStr" : "SECONDARY",
            "uptime" : 87,
            "optime" : {
                "t" : 1397231918000,
                "i" : 1
            },
            "optimeDate" : ISODate("2014-04-11T15:58:38Z"),
            "lastHeartbeat" : ISODate("2014-04-11T15:59:25Z"),
            "pingMs" : 0
        },
        {
            "_id" : 2,
            "name" : "mongod3.replicaset.com:27017",
            "health" : 1,
            "state" : 2,
            "stateStr" : "SECONDARY",
            "uptime" : 48,
            "optime" : {
                "t" : 1397231918000,
                "i" : 1
            },
            "optimeDate" : ISODate("2014-04-11T15:58:38Z"),
            "lastHeartbeat" : ISODate("2014-04-11T15:59:24Z"),
            "pingMs" : 0
        }
    ],
    "ok" : 1
}
```

As you can see, we have a replica set with three members, one primary and two secondaries. The `stateStr` property in the `rs.status()` output shows the status of each member in the replica set, that is, for mongod2.replicaset.com and the secondary member, mongod3.replicset.com.

Also, you can simply run the `rs.status()` command in the secondary mongo shell to check the status of the replica set.

Removing a member

In order to remove a member from an existing replica set, you can use the following command:

```
rs.remove("mongod2.replicaset.com:27017")
```

To remove a node, you should introduce both the hostname and port number to the remove method. After executing the command, you should see the result shown in the following screenshot:

```
PRIMARY> rs.remove("mongod2.replicaset.com:27017")
{ "ok" : 1 }
```

To confirm that the member has been removed successfully, you can simply issue the `rs.status()` command again.

Adding an arbiter

An `arbiter` node doesn't store any data and only has a vote in replica set election. If you have a replica set with an even number of members, you should add an arbiter.

Because an arbiter doesn't store data, to boost the performance of an arbiter, you can disable some features safely. This can be done by performing the following steps:

1. To run an arbiter, create the `dbpath` directory first. This directory isn't used to hold data; instead it is used to store configurations. This can be done with the following command line:

    ```
    mkdir /data/arbiter
    ```

2. Next, run the `mongod` instance using the created `dbpath` directory:

    ```
    mongod --port 20000 --dbpath /data/arbiter --replSet rs1
    ```

As in the case of secondary or primary nodes, you can use the configuration file instead of command-line parameters to run the arbiter instance. It's recommended that you use this approach.

3. After starting the arbiter node, you can add it to the replica set simply by executing the following command in the mongo shell:

```
rs.addArb("arbiter1.replicaset.com:20000")
```

4. After executing the preceding command, you should see the result shown in the following screenshot:

```
rs1:PRIMARY> rs.addArb("arbiter1.replicaset.com:20000")
{ "ok" : 1 }
```

5. Furthermore, to check the arbiter's status, you can use the same rs.status() command. The following screenshot illustrates the status of our arbiter:

```
{
        "_id" : 3,
        "name" : "arbiter1.replicaset.com:20000",
        "health" : 1,
        "state" : 0,
        "stateStr" : "STARTUP",
        "uptime" : 9,
        "lastHeartbeat" : ISODate("2014-04-11T21:16:37Z"),
        "lastHeartbeatRecv" : ISODate("1970-01-01T00:00:00Z"),
        "pingMs" : 0
}
```

Failover testing

In this section, we will deactivate the specific nodes to force the replica set to make an election and change the nodes' role.

First of all, we will deactivate one of the secondary nodes by stopping the mongod service on the secondary machine.

Right after stopping the service of `mongod3.replicaset.com`, the replica set will set this node as an unreachable secondary node, as shown in the following screenshot:

```
PRIMARY> rs.status()
{
        "set" : "rs1",
        "date" : ISODate("2014-04-11T20:34:48Z"),
        "myState" : 1,
        "members" : [
                {
                        "_id" : 0,
                        "name" : "mongod1.replicaset.com:27017",
                        "health" : 1,
                        "state" : 1,
                        "stateStr" : "PRIMARY",
                        "optime" : {
                                "t" : 1397231918000,
                                "i" : 1
                        },
                        "optimeDate" : ISODate("2014-04-11T15:58:38Z"),
                        "self" : true
                },
                {

                        "_id" : 1,
                        "name" : "mongod2.replicaset.com:27017",
                        "health" : 1,
                        "state" : 2,
                        "stateStr" : "SECONDARY",
                        "uptime" : 54,
                        "optime" : {
                                "t" : 1397231918000,
                                "i" : 1
                        },
                        "optimeDate" : ISODate("2014-04-11T15:58:38Z"),
                        "lastHeartbeat" : ISODate("2014-04-11T20:34:46Z"),
                        "pingMs" : 0,
                        "errmsg" : "syncing to: mongod1.replicaset.com:27017"
                },
                {

                        "_id" : 2,
                        "name" : "mongod3.replicaset.com:27017",
                        "health" : 0,
                        "state" : 8,
                        "stateStr" : "(not reachable/healthy)",
                        "uptime" : 0,
                        "optime" : {
                                "t" : 1397231918000,
                                "i" : 1
                        },
                        "optimeDate" : ISODate("2014-04-11T15:58:38Z"),
                        "lastHeartbeat" : ISODate("2014-04-11T20:34:40Z"),
                        "pingMs" : 0,
                        "errmsg" : "socket exception"
                }
        ],
```

The status of the replica set shows that the third member has an issue, so this member becomes unavailable until the replica set gets a ping from it. After starting the service again, the members' status changes again as shown in the following screenshot:

```
{
    "_id" : 2,
    "name" : "mongod3.replicaset.com:27017",
    "health" : 1,
    "state" : 2,
    "stateStr" : "SECONDARY",
    "uptime" : 1,
    "optime" : {
            "t" : 1397231918000,
            "i" : 1
    },
    "optimeDate" : ISODate("2014-04-11T15:58:38Z"),
    "lastHeartbeat" : ISODate("2014-04-11T20:41:40Z"),
    "pingMs" : 1
}
```

 Network issues or hardware failure on the member's machine also has the same result as stopping the MongoDB service.

For the next test, we will halt the primary node's service. After stopping the service in the `primary` node, the replica set uses an election process to choose the next `primary` node from `secondary` nodes.

In the following diagram, you can see the `rs.status()` output after stopping the `primary` node (the hostname is `mongod1.replicaset.com`):

```
{
                "_id" : 1,
                "name" : "mongod2.replicaset.com:27017",
                "health" : 1,
                "state" : 2,
                "stateStr" : "SECONDARY",
                "uptime" : 290,
                "optime" : Timestamp(1397231918, 1),
                "optimeDate" : ISODate("2014-04-11T15:58:38Z"),
                "lastHeartbeat" : ISODate("2014-04-11T20:46:28Z"),
                "lastHeartbeatRecv" : ISODate("2014-04-11T20:46:29Z"),
                "pingMs" : 4,
                "lastHeartbeatMessage" : "syncing to: mongod3.replicaset.
com:27017",
                "syncingTo" : "mongod3.replicaset.com:27017"
        },
        {
                "_id" : 2,
                "name" : "mongod3.replicaset.com:27017",
                "health" : 1,
                "state" : 1,
                "stateStr" : "PRIMARY",
                "uptime" : 290,
                "optime" : Timestamp(1397231918, 1),
                "optimeDate" : ISODate("2014-04-11T15:58:38Z"),
                "self" : true
        }
    ],
    "ok" : 1
```

As you can see in the preceding screenshot, other `secondary` nodes will sync their data to the new `primary` node. In our example, the next `primary` node is `mongod3.replicaset.com`.

Also, you can see the previous `primary` node's status in the following screenshot:

```
{
        "_id" : 0,
        "name" : "mongod1.replicaset.com:27017",
        "health" : 0,
        "state" : 8,
        "stateStr" : "(not reachable/healthy)",
        "uptime" : 0,
        "optime" : Timestamp(1397231918, 1),
        "optimeDate" : ISODate("2014-04-11T15:58:38Z"),
        "lastHeartbeat" : ISODate("2014-04-11T20:46:28Z"),
        "lastHeartbeatRecv" : ISODate("2014-04-11T20:45:14Z"),
        "pingMs" : 0
},
```

To complete our testing scenario, we will start the `mongod1.replicaset.com` service again.

Right after enabling the service, `mongod` will send ping or heartbeat messages to the current `primary` node, and also, the replica set sets its status to the `secondary` node.

In the following diagram, you can see the result of enabling the `mongod` service again:

```
"members" : [
        {
                "_id" : 0,
                "name" : "mongod1.replicaset.com:27017",
                "health" : 1,
                "state" : 2,
                "stateStr" : "SECONDARY",
                "uptime" : 2,
                "optime" : Timestamp(1397231918, 1),
                "optimeDate" : ISODate("2014-04-11T15:58:38Z"),
                "lastHeartbeat" : ISODate("2014-04-11T20:55:55Z"),
                "lastHeartbeatRecv" : ISODate("2014-04-11T20:45:14Z"),
                "pingMs" : 0
        },
        {
                "_id" : 1,
                "name" : "mongod2.replicaset.com:27017",
                "health" : 1,
                "state" : 2,
                "stateStr" : "SECONDARY",
                "uptime" : 858,
                "optime" : Timestamp(1397231918, 1),
                "optimeDate" : ISODate("2014-04-11T15:58:38Z"),
                "lastHeartbeat" : ISODate("2014-04-11T20:55:56Z"),
                "lastHeartbeatRecv" : ISODate("2014-04-11T20:55:55Z"),
                "pingMs" : 0,
                "syncingTo" : "mongod3.replicaset.com:27017"
        },
```

Please note that after enabling the service, mongod1 won't become primary again. The status will be secondary until the next election, then if it receives the majority of the votes, it will become the primary again.

Summary

In this chapter, we studied how to create a replica set from scratch to provide a readily available MongoDB server. First of all, we discussed the basic considerations of a replica set. Next, we configured the workspace to run the replica set. Additionally, we learned basic replica set commands in order to add or remove members from the replica set.

In our example, we had a three-member replica set, one primary and two secondary nodes. After configuration and setup, to test the replica set, we deactivated different nodes in the replica set. Also, we found that upon disabling the primary node, the replica set will choose another primary node from the active secondary members using an election process.

Also, we learned to run an arbiter node and add it to an existing replica set network. We found that arbiter nodes won't save and hold data at all.

In the next chapter, we will learn sharding in MongoDB, and distributing a dataset into different servers and machines.

6
Understanding the Concept of Sharding

After learning about replication and replica sets, we can jump into the more complex concepts of MongoDB. In this chapter, we will talk about one of the most valuable MongoDB features, that is, **sharding**. Using this feature, you can spread your data across different servers to distribute operation pressure between different machines and provide better performance.

In this chapter, we will learn the basic terms and concepts of sharding. In the next chapter, we will configure and set up a server from scratch.

Understanding scaling

When you are using MongoDB in a production environment and under high throughput, you may face a lack of server resources. Storing large datasets on a single machine can be the biggest problem. In addition, responding to a lot of read/write requests from different clients can be a concern because these kinds of processes are resource-consuming and can exhaust the server's resources.

To address these problems, scale your database system to support more clients. Basically, there are two ways to scale a system, **vertical scaling** and **horizontal scaling**.

In the vertical scaling approach, the system administrator will add more resources and capacities to an existing server. However, adding more capacity to an existing system has some limitations, making this approach less useful. Adding more CPU cores or RAM capacity to a machine can be more expensive than setting up a new smaller machine. Meanwhile, some cloud-based service providers don't offer very large capacity machines so you have to use smaller instances. On the other hand, using separate machines reduces the risk of failure of a single instance.

On other hand, the horizontal scaling method increases the capacity of the entire server by merging smaller instances together. For instance, in order to have an entire server with 4 GB of RAM, we need four different machines each with a 1 GB RAM capacity.

Despite the difficulty in maintaining independent machines, this approach costs less than vertical scaling and protects the entire system from failure if a single server encounters a hardware crash.

The following diagram shows the difference between vertical and horizontal scaling:

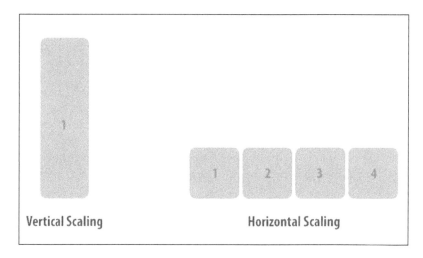

Each box represents a separate server. In vertical scaling, we have a single server with more capacity, but in horizontal scaling, we use separate servers and link them to each other in order to build more capacity.

Learning about sharding

The good news is that MongoDB has come up with a clever solution to scale your database system easily. Sharding is a technique used to scale a database horizontally.

Using sharding, the entire database is divided into separate single databases on different machines. Finally, using a query router, all the separate nodes make a single logical database.

Let's look at an example of sharding. Suppose we have a database sized 1 TB. Storing such a large dataset on a single server is a big challenge, so we use sharding to divide the entire database into smaller instances called **shards**.

In order to reduce the size of the entire database, we divide it into databases sized 256 GB. During the sharding procedure, each part of the database is divided using a shard key and other options that configure settings for shards such as the size of the dataset.

The following diagram illustrates the example of a 1 TB database being sharded across four instances:

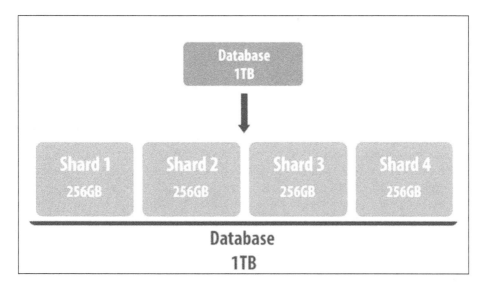

The benefits of using sharding are not limited to reducing the size of the database and dividing it among smaller instances. With the help of sharding, you can support a higher amount of requests from clients and improve the database performance as well.

The idea is that a client needs to access a single instance or shard when writing data, and not the entire database. Hence, clients request routes to different shards and machines instead of a single database and machine. As a result, the entire database can now support more requests.

In the next sections, we will detail how to choose a shard key and set up sharding for a database.

Understanding sharding modules

In order to establish sharding for a database in MongoDB, we need to use some different modules and components. Each module is responsible for a specific task.

The first module to study is a shard. Each shard, whether a single mongod instance or a replica set, is responsible for storing data in a machine. We recommend that you use a replica set as a shard in a production environment, but you can use a single mongod instance for development and testing environments.

The next component is a query router. The query router's task is to get all requests from applications and clients, route them to the corresponding shard, and finally, return the result to the client. This module is the only interface that has clients and all applications interact with it. The sharded cluster can include one or more query routers and adding more query routers can improve the sharded cluster's performance because user requests will be divided between query routers. However, note that adding more query routers than shards increases latency because all query routers perform routing to a single shard. The mongos process is the query router module that routes requests from clients.

The last module is the configuration server. This module collects metadata about sharded clusters, shard configurations, each node status, and the relationship between them. With the help of this module, query routers can send requests to correct nodes and shards. In a production environment, the sharded cluster has three configuration servers. However, in some situations, one or two configuration servers might be unavailable, although at least one configuration server must be available to have a functional sharded cluster.

The following diagram shows a sharded cluster and the relationship between each component:

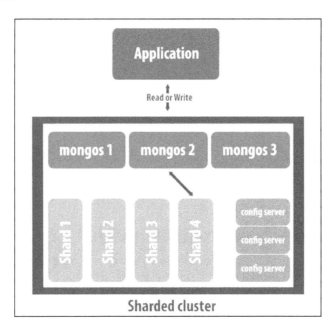

In the preceding diagram, we have three query routers, four shards, and three configuration servers.

Utilizing a sharding key

A sharded cluster uses a shard key to divide and partition the entire dataset into smaller pieces. A shard key is an indexed key or indexed compound key that exists in all records in the collection. After defining the shard key and the size of each chunk, the engine splits the dataset into smaller chunks and syncs them with shards.

Mainly, a shard key can be either range-based or hash-based. Using range-based keys, MongoDB divides the dataset into specific ranges. In hash-based keys, the engine creates hashes from the given field and divides the dataset using those hashes. In the next chapter, we will use both methods to create shard key using real-world examples.

In the next section, we will talk about each technique in detail.

Understanding range-based keys

One of the methods to define a key is to use a range-based mechanism. Using range-based keys, the database engine splits the dataset into smaller parts with specific ranges of the given field's value.

For instance, you have a field that has numeric value and value ranges between 0 and 100. By introducing this field and configuring chunk sizes to four chunks, you will have four shards and the first chunk's data starts from the minimum value of the introduced field; the last chunk ends with the maximum value of the field.

The following diagram illustrates the usage of range-based keys in a sharded cluster:

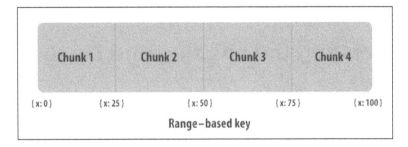

 In this method, records with closed value of the introduced field are likely to be in the same chunk and consequently, in the same shard.

Understanding hash-based keys

In this method, the engine uses the given key to make hashes from it using the hash function. Then, by requesting clients to fetch data, MongoDB uses the hash function to find the location of each hash key in shards and then routes the client to the correct shard. This technique ensures that collections are randomly divided between shards and chunks.

The following diagram shows a sharded cluster that uses hash-based keys to split the dataset:

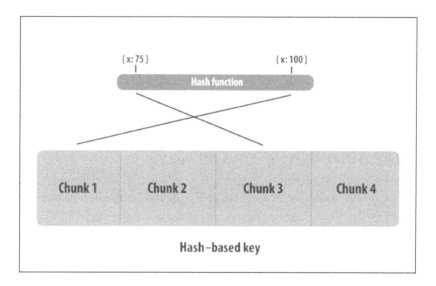

 Using the hash-based method, documents with a close value of the given field are unlikely to be in the same chunk and thus, the same shard.

Understanding the splitting and balancing processes

Splitting and balancing are two background processes that perform the maintenance of an entire cluster. The splitting process prevents chunks from growing too large and controls the size of each chunk. When a chunk size grows larger than the defined chunk size, the engine splits that chunk in half.

The default size of the chunk is 64 MB, but you can change the size by overwriting configurations. Suppose a chunk grows more than 64 MB, the splitting processes make two new chunks at half of the size of the parent chunk.

The following diagram shows the procedure of dividing a chunk into new chunks:

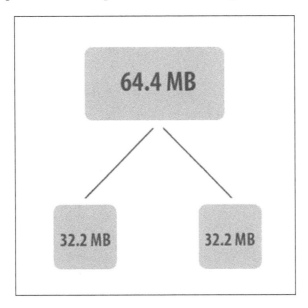

In the preceding diagram, a chunk grows more than 64 MB so the splitting processes divide it into two 32.2 MB chunks.

 The splitting process doesn't manage the migration of chunks and is only responsible for making new chunks.

On the other hand, the balancing process task is to migrate chunks from one shard to another. When the number of chunks in a shard is not properly sorted and doesn't have the appropriate number of chunks, the balancing process migrates the chunk from a shard that has a larger number of chunks to one that has the least amount.

In migration, the chunk migrates to the destination shard from the origin shard. MongoDB then removes the chunk from the origin shard only when the migration is successfully completed.

While migrating, queries to the target chunk route to the origin shard, so it prevents data loss and failures.

The following diagram illustrates the procedure of migration from origin to the destination shard:

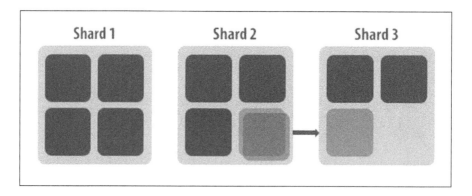

In the preceding diagram, because shard 2 has more than four chunks, balancing processes move a chunk to shard 3 to balance the number of chunks among all the shards.

Summary

In this chapter, you learned the basic terms, concepts, and components of creating a sharded cluster and using the sharding technique in MongoDB. First, we discussed the different methods of scaling a database system, vertical and horizontal scaling. Then, we introduced the sharding method, which is the horizontal scaling solution for MongoDB.

Also, you learned about the different parts and components of sharding, shards, query routers, and configuration servers. Next, you learned one of the important parts of the sharding procedure, the shard key. Then, all the techniques available to define a shard key were introduced and in the next section, we talked about performance difference between methods. Furthermore, we discussed splitting and balancing processes, which help with maintenance and retention of the balance of data size and chunks in the shards.

In the next chapter, we will configure and establish a sharded cluster from scratch using terms and concepts that we have learned up until now.

7
Sharding in Action

In the previous chapters, we learned the basic terms of sharding in MongoDB. Also, we discussed the replica set feature and how it can be used in action and real-world examples. Now, we know enough and can establish sharding on an existing database or single collection. In this chapter, we will connect different machines together, enable the sharding feature on a database, and see the results using screenshots and pictures.

Preparing the environment

Before jumping into configuring and setting up the cluster network, we have to check some parameters and prepare the environment.

To enable sharding for a database or collection, we have to configure some configuration servers that hold the cluster network metadata and shards information. Other parts of the cluster network use these configuration servers to get information about other shards.

In production, it's recommended to have exactly three configuration servers on different machines. The reason for establishing each shard on a different server is to improve the safety of data and nodes. If one of the machines crashes, the whole cluster won't be unavailable.

For the testing and developing environment, you can host all the configuration servers on a single server. Besides, we have two more parts for our cluster network, shards and mongos, or query routers. Query routers are the interface for all clients. All read/write requests are routed to this module. The query router or mongos instance, using configuration servers, route the request to the corresponding shard.

The following diagram shows the cluster network, modules, and the relationship between them:

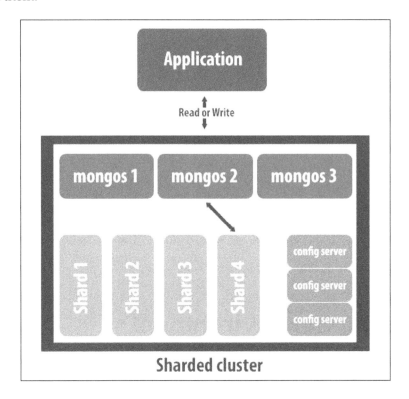

 It's important that all modules and parts have network access and are able to connect to each other. If you have firewall, you should configure it correctly and give proper access to all cluster modules.

Each configuration server has an address that routes to the target machine. We have exactly three configuration servers in our example, and the following list shows the hostnames:

- cfg1.sharding.com
- cfg2.sharding.com
- cfg3.sharding.com

In our example, because we are going to set up a demo of the sharding feature, we deploy all configuration servers on a single machine with different ports. This means all configuration server addresses point to the same server, but we use different ports to establish the configuration server.

For production use, all things will be the same, except you need to host the configuration servers on separate machines.

In the next section, we will implement all parts of the configuration server and finally connect all of them together to start the sharding server and run the cluster network.

Implementing configuration servers

Now it's time to start the first part of sharding. Establishing a configuration server is as easy as running a mongod instance using the --configsvr parameter.

The following scheme shows the structure of the command:

```
mongod --configsvr --dbpath <path> --port <port>
```

If you don't pass the dbpath or port parameters, the configuration server uses /data/configdb as the path to store data and port 27019 to execute the instance. However, you can override the default values using the preceding command.

If this is the first time that you have run the configuration server, you might be faced with some issues due to the existence of dbpath. Before running the configuration server, make sure that you have created the path; otherwise, you will see an error as shown in the following screenshot:

```
Tue Apr 29 23:30:00 [initandlisten] options: { configsvr: true }
Tue Apr 29 23:30:00 [initandlisten] exception in initAndListen: 10296 dbpath (/data/configdb) does not exist, terminating
Tue Apr 29 23:30:00 dbexit:
Tue Apr 29 23:30:00 [initandlisten] shutdown: going to close listening sockets...
Tue Apr 29 23:30:00 [initandlisten] shutdown: going to flush diaglog...
Tue Apr 29 23:30:00 [initandlisten] shutdown: going to close sockets...
Tue Apr 29 23:30:00 [initandlisten] shutdown: waiting for fs preallocator...
Tue Apr 29 23:30:00 [initandlisten] shutdown: lock for final commit...
Tue Apr 29 23:30:00 [initandlisten] shutdown: final commit...
Tue Apr 29 23:30:00 [initandlisten] shutdown: closing all files...
Tue Apr 29 23:30:00 [initandlisten] closeAllFiles() finished
Tue Apr 29 23:30:00 dbexit: really exiting now
```

You can simply create the directory using the mkdir command as shown in the following line of command:

```
mkdir /data/configdb
```

Also, make sure that you are executing the instance with a sufficient permission level; otherwise, you will get an error as shown in the following screenshot:

```
Tue Apr 29 23:46:17 [initandlisten] options: { configsvr: true }
Tue Apr 29 23:46:17 [initandlisten] exception in initAndListen: 10309 Unable to create/open lock file: /data/configdb/mongod.lock err
no:13 Permission denied Is a mongod instance already running?, terminating
Tue Apr 29 23:46:17 dbexit:
Tue Apr 29 23:46:17 [initandlisten] shutdown: going to close listening sockets...
Tue Apr 29 23:46:17 [initandlisten] shutdown: going to flush diaglog...
Tue Apr 29 23:46:17 [initandlisten] shutdown: going to close sockets...
Tue Apr 29 23:46:17 [initandlisten] shutdown: waiting for fs preallocator...
Tue Apr 29 23:46:17 [initandlisten] shutdown: lock for final commit...
Tue Apr 29 23:46:17 [initandlisten] shutdown: final commit...
Tue Apr 29 23:46:17 [initandlisten] shutdown: closing all files...
Tue Apr 29 23:46:17 [initandlisten] closeAllFiles() finished
Tue Apr 29 23:46:17 [initandlisten] shutdown: removing fs lock...
Tue Apr 29 23:46:17 [initandlisten] couldn't remove fs lock errno:9 Bad file descriptor
Tue Apr 29 23:46:17 dbexit: really exiting now
```

The problem is that the `mongod` instance can't create the lock file because of the lack of permissions. To address this issue, you should simply execute the command using a root or administrator permission level.

After executing the command using the proper permission level, you should see a result like the following screenshot:

```
→ bin  sudo mongod --configsvr
Tue Apr 29 23:56:15 [initandlisten] MongoDB starting : pid=3964 port=27019 dbpath=/data/configdb 64-bit host=cfg1.sharding.com
Tue Apr 29 23:56:15 [initandlisten] db version v2.0.0, pdfile version 4.5
Tue Apr 29 23:56:15 [initandlisten] git version: 695c67dff0ffc361b8568a13366f027caa406222
Tue Apr 29 23:56:15 [initandlisten] build info: Darwin erh2.10gen.cc 9.6.0 Darwin Kernel Version 9.6.0: Mon Nov 24 17:37:00 PST 2008;
    root:xnu-1228.9.59~1/RELEASE_I386 i386 BOOST_LIB_VERSION=1_40
Tue Apr 29 23:56:15 [initandlisten] options: { configsvr: true }
Tue Apr 29 23:56:15 [initandlisten] journal dir=/data/configdb/journal
Tue Apr 29 23:56:15 [initandlisten] recover : no journal files present, no recovery needed
Tue Apr 29 23:56:15 [websvr] admin web console waiting for connections on port 28019
Tue Apr 29 23:56:15 [initandlisten] waiting for connections on port 27019
```

As you can see now, we have a configuration server for the hostname `cfg1.sharding.com` with port `27019` and with `dbpath` as `/data/configdb`.

Also, there is a web console to watch and control the configuration server running on port `28019`. By pointing the web browser to the address `http://localhost:28019/`, you can see the console.

The following screenshot shows a part of this web console:

---

mongod cfg1.sharding.com:27019

List all commands | Replica set status

Commands: buildInfo cursorInfo features isMaster listDatabases replSetGetStatus serverStatus top

```
db version v2.0.0, pdfile version 4.5
git hash: 695c67dff0ffc361b8568a13366f027caa406222
sys info: Darwin erh2.10gen.cc 9.6.0 Darwin Kernel Version 9.6.0: Mon Nov 24 17:37:00 PST 2008; root:xnu-1228.9.59~1/RELEASE_I386 i386 BOOST_LIB_VERSION=1_40
uptime: 137 seconds
```

low level requires read lock

```
time to get readlock: 0ms
# databases: 1

replication:
master: 0
slave: 0
```

Now we have the first configuration server up and running. With the same method, you can launch other instances, that is, using `/data/configdb2` with port `27020` for the second configuration server, and `/data/configdb3` with port `27021` for the third configuration server.

Configuring a mongos instance

After configuring the configuration servers, we should bind them to the core module of clustering. The `mongos` instance is responsible for binding all modules and parts together to make a complete sharding core.

This module is simple and lightweight, and we can host it on the same machine that hosts other modules, such as configuration servers. It doesn't need a separate directory to store data. The `mongos` process uses port `27017` by default, but you can change the port using the configuration parameters.

To define the configuration servers, you can use the configuration file or command-line parameters. Create a new file using your text editor in the `/etc/` directory and add the following configuring settings:

```
configdb = cfg1.sharding.com:27019, cfg2.sharding.com:27020 cfg3.
sharding.com:27021
```

To execute and run the `mongos` instance, you can simply use the following command:

```
mongos -f /etc/mongos.conf
```

After executing the command, you should see an output like the following screenshot:

```
➜  ~ mongos -f /etc/mongos.conf
Thu May  1 10:20:27 mongos db version v2.0.0, pdfile version 4.5 starting (--help for usage)
Thu May  1 10:20:27 git version: 695c67dff0ffc361b8568a13366f027caa406222
Thu May  1 10:20:27 build info: Darwin erh2.10gen.cc 9.6.0 Darwin Kernel Version 9.6.0: Mon Nov 24 17:37:00 PST 2008; root:xnu-1228.9.5
9~1/RELEASE_I386 i386 BOOST_LIB_VERSION=1_40
Thu May  1 10:20:27 SyncClusterConnection connecting to [cfg1.sharding.com:27019]
Thu May  1 10:20:27 SyncClusterConnection connecting to [cfg2.sharding.com:27020]
Thu May  1 10:20:27 SyncClusterConnection connecting to [cfg3.sharding.com:27021]
Thu May  1 10:20:27 SyncClusterConnection connecting to [cfg1.sharding.com:27019]
Thu May  1 10:20:27 SyncClusterConnection connecting to [cfg2.sharding.com:27020]
Thu May  1 10:20:27 SyncClusterConnection connecting to [cfg3.sharding.com:27021]
Thu May  1 10:20:40 [Balancer] about to contact config servers and shards
Thu May  1 10:20:40 [websvr] admin web console waiting for connections on port 28017
Thu May  1 10:20:40 [mongosMain] waiting for connections on port 27017
Thu May  1 10:20:40 [Balancer] config servers and shards contacted successfully
```

 Please note that if you have a configuration server that has been already used in a different sharding network, you can't use the existing data directory. You should create a new and empty data directory for the configuration server.

Currently, we have mongos and all configuration servers that work together pretty well. In the next section, we will add shards to the mongos instance to complete the whole network.

Managing a mongos instance

Now it's time to add shards and split the entire dataset into smaller pieces. For production use, each shard should be a replica set network, but for the development and testing environment, you can simply add a single mongod instance to the cluster. In previous chapters, we learned how to set up and configure a replica set from scratch.

To control and manage the mongos instance, we can simply use the mongo shell to connect to the mongos and execute commands. To connect to the mongos instance, you use the following command:

```
mongo --host <mongos hostname> --port <mongos port>
```

For instance, our mongos address is mongos1.sharding.com and the port is 27017. This is depicted in the following screenshot:

```
➜  ~  mongo --host mongos1.sharding.com --port 27017
MongoDB shell version: 2.0.0
connecting to: mongos1.sharding.com:27017/test
mongos>
```

After connecting to the mongos instance, we have a command environment, and we can use it to add, remove, or modify shards, or even get the status of the entire sharding network.

Using the following command, you can get the status of the sharding network:

```
sh.status()
```

The following screenshot illustrates the output of this command:

```
mongos> sh.status()
--- Sharding Status ---
  sharding version: { "_id" : 1, "version" : 3 }
  shards:
  databases:
        { "_id" : "admin", "partitioned" : false, "primary" : "config" }

Thu May  1 11:29:59 uncaught exception: error { "$err" : "can't find a shard to put new db on", "code" : 10185 }
mongos>
```

Because we haven't added any shards to sharding, you see an error that says there are no shards in the sharding network.

Using the `sh.help()` command, you can see all commands as shown in the following screenshot:

```
mongos> sh.help()
        sh.addShard( host )                         server:port OR setname/server:port
        sh.enableSharding(dbname)                   enables sharding on the database dbname
        sh.shardCollection(fullName,key,unique)     shards the collection
        sh.splitFind(fullName,find)                 splits the chunk that find is in at the median
        sh.splitAt(fullName,middle)                 splits the chunk that middle is in at middle
        sh.moveChunk(fullName,find,to)              move the chunk where 'find' is to 'to' (name of shard)
        sh.setBalancerState( <bool on or not> )     turns the balancer on or off true=on, false=off
        sh.getBalancerState()                       return true if on, off if not
        sh.isBalancerRunning()                      return true if the balancer is running on any mongos
        sh.status()                                 prints a general overview of the cluster
```

Using the `sh.addShard()` function, you can add shards to the network.

Adding shards to mongos

After connecting to the `mongos` instance, you can add shards to sharding. Basically, you can add two types of endpoints to the `mongos` as a shard; a replica set or a standalone `mongod` instance.

MongoDB has a `sh` namespace and a function called `addShard()`, which is used to add a new shard to an existing sharding network. Here is the example of a command to add a new shard. This is shown in the following screenshot:

```
sh.addShard( host )                         server:port OR setname/server:port
```

To add a replica set to `mongos` you should follow this scheme:

`setname/server:port`

For instance, if you have a replica set with the name of `rs1`, hostname `mongod1.replicaset.com`, and port number `27017`, the command will be as follows:

`sh.addShard("rs1/mongod1.replicaset.com:27017")`

Using the same function, we can add standalone `mongod` instances. So, if we have a `mongod` instance with the hostname `mongod1.sharding.com` listening on port `27017`, the command will be as follows:

`sh.addShard("mongod1.sharding.com:27017")`

You can use a secondary or primary hostname to add the replica set as a shard to the sharding network. MongoDB will detect the primary and use the `primary` node to interact with sharding.

Now, we add the replica set network that we made in the previous chapters to sharding using the following command:

```
sh.addShard("rs1/mongod1.replicaset.com:27017")
```

If everything goes well, you won't see any output from the console, which means the adding process was successful. This is shown in the following screenshot:

```
mongos> sh.addShard("rs1/mongod1.replicaset.com:27017")
```

To see the status of sharding, you can use the `sh.status()` command. This is demonstrated in the following screenshot:

```
mongos> sh.status()
--- Sharding Status ---
  sharding version: { "_id" : 1, "version" : 3 }
  shards:
        {  "_id" : "rs1",  "host" : "rs1/mongod1.replicaset.com:27017,mongod3.replicaset.com:27017,mongod2.replicaset.com:2
7017" }
  databases:
        {  "_id" : "admin",  "partitioned" : false,  "primary" : "config" }
        {  "_id" : "test",  "partitioned" : false,  "primary" : "rs1" }

mongos>
```

Next, we will establish another standalone `mongod` instance and add it to the sharding process. The port number of `mongod` is `27016` and the hostname is `mongod1.sharding.com`.

The following screenshot shows the output after starting the new `mongod` instance:

```
→ ~ sudo mongod --port 27016 --dbpath /data/mongod5
Thu May  1 14:00:44 [initandlisten] MongoDB starting : pid=12447 port=27016 dbpath=/data/mongod5 64-bit host=Afshin-Mehraba
nis-MacBook-Pro-5.local
Thu May  1 14:00:44 [initandlisten] db version v2.0.0, pdfile version 4.5
Thu May  1 14:00:44 [initandlisten] git version: 695c67dff0ffc361b8568a13366f027caa406222
Thu May  1 14:00:44 [initandlisten] build info: Darwin erh2.10gen.cc 9.6.0 Darwin Kernel Version 9.6.0: Mon Nov 24 17:37:00
 PST 2008; root:xnu-1228.9.59~1/RELEASE_I386 i386 BOOST_LIB_VERSION=1_40
Thu May  1 14:00:44 [initandlisten] options: { dbpath: "/data/mongod5", port: 27016 }
Thu May  1 14:00:44 [initandlisten] journal dir=/data/mongod5/journal
Thu May  1 14:00:44 [initandlisten] recover : no journal files present, no recovery needed
Thu May  1 14:00:44 [websvr] admin web console waiting for connections on port 28016
Thu May  1 14:00:44 [initandlisten] waiting for connections on port 27016
```

Chapter 7

Using the same approach, we will add the preceding node to the sharding process. This is shown in the following screenshot:

```
mongos> sh.addShard("mongod1.sharding.com:27016")
mongos>
```

It's time to see the sharding status using the `sh.status()` command:

```
mongos> sh.status()
--- Sharding Status ---
  sharding version: { "_id" : 1, "version" : 3 }
  shards:
        {  "_id" : "rs1",  "host" : "rs1/mongod1.replicaset.com:27017,mongod3.replicaset.com:27017,mongod2.replicaset.com:2
7017" }
        {  "_id" : "shard0000",  "host" : "mongod1.sharding.com:27016" }
  databases:
        {  "_id" : "admin",  "partitioned" : false,  "primary" : "config" }
        {  "_id" : "test",  "partitioned" : false,  "primary" : "rs1" }

mongos>
```

As you can see in the preceding screenshot, now we have two shards. The first one is a replica set with the name `rs1`, and the second shard is a standalone `mongod` instance on port `27016`.

If you create a new database on each shard, MongoDB syncs this new database with the `mongos` instance. Using the `show dbs` command, you can see all databases from all shards as shown in the following screenshot:

```
mongos> show dbs
config  0.1875GB
newdb   0.203125GB
rsdb    0.203125GB
test    0.20312500093132257GB
mongos>
```

> The **configuration database** is an internal database that MongoDB uses to configure and manage the sharding network.

Currently, we have all the sharding modules working together. The last and final step is to enable sharding for a database and a collection.

[81]

Enable sharding

In order to enable sharding for a collection of data, we should enable sharding for a database first.

We should use the same `mongo` command-line environment to enable, deactivate, or modify database sharding. To enable sharding for a database, you can use following command:

sh.enableSharding(database)

We enable sharding for the database `newdb`. This is shown in the following screenshot:

```
mongos> sh.enableSharding("newdb")
{ "ok" : 1 }
mongos>
```

If the enabling process is successful, you get the preceding message from the shell. Otherwise, you will get an error. Now that we enabled sharding for the database, the next step is to enable sharding for database collections.

The following screenshot shows the status of sharding after enabling sharding for the `newdb` database:

```
mongos> sh.status()
--- Sharding Status ---
  sharding version: { "_id" : 1, "version" : 3 }
  shards:
      { "_id" : "rs1",  "host" : "rs1/mongod1.replicaset.com:27017,mongod3.replicaset.com:27017,mongod2.replicaset.com:2
7017" }
      { "_id" : "shard0000",  "host" : "mongod1.sharding.com:27016" }
  databases:
      { "_id" : "admin",  "partitioned" : false,  "primary" : "config" }
      { "_id" : "test",   "partitioned" : false,  "primary" : "rs1" }
      { "_id" : "newdb",  "partitioned" : true,   "primary" : "shard0000" }

mongos>
```

As you can see in the preceding screenshot, the partitioned field is `true` for the database `newdb`, but it's `false` for other databases.

Before jumping into enabling sharding for a collection of databases, you should consider one or more shard keys. MongoDB will distribute the whole dataset using these keys in different shards. This is called a sharding strategy (read the previous chapter to learn more about sharding keys and its different types).

Suppose the `newdb` database has a `test` collection with the following schema:

```
{
    "_id": ObjectId("725c211a412f812548cv3258"),
    "data": 1
}
```

We are going to enable sharding for this collection on the field `_id`. MongoDB will distribute the data across available shards with the `_id` field.

Simply by issuing the following command, you can enable sharding for a collection:

```
sh.shardCollection("database.collection", shard-keys)
```

But, before enabling sharding for a collection using the hash-based key strategy, you need to create an index on the collection for the shard key using the following command:

```
db.test.ensureIndex( { _id : "hashed" } )
```

The result of issuing the preceding command would be as shown in the following screenshot:

```
mongos> db.test.ensureIndex( { _id : "hashed" } )
{
        "raw" : {
                "mongod1.sharding.com:27016" : {
                        "note" : "downgraded",
                        "sentTo" : "mongod1.sharding.com:27016",
                        "eachIndex" : [
                                {
                                        "spec" : {
                                                "key" : {
                                                        "_id" : "hashed"
                                                },
                                                "name" : "_id_hashed",
                                                "ns" : "newdb.test"
                                        },
                                        "gle" : {
                                                "n" : 0,
                                                "connectionId" : 15,
                                                "err" : null,
                                                "ok" : 1
                                        }
                                }
                        ],
                        "ok" : 1
                }
        },
        "ok" : 1
}
mongos>
```

Consequently, we can enable sharding for the collection and the `_id` field. In our example, the command is as follows:

```
sh.shardCollection("newdb.test", { "_id": "hashed" } )
```

The following screenshot shows the output of issuing this command:

```
mongos> sh.shardCollection("newdb.test", { "_id": "hashed" } )
{ "collectionsharded" : "newdb.test", "ok" : 1 }
mongos>
```

It's not necessary to enable sharding only for existing collections; you can enable sharding for a collection that doesn't exist yet. MongoDB will create indexes on the collection using defined fields in the shardCollection() function.

If the collection already exists and contains data, you need to add indexes for the shard keys using the ensureIndex() function first. The same approach should be used to add a shard key with the hash-based method.

After enabling sharding on test collection, our sharding status is shown in the following screenshot:

```
shards:
    {  "_id" : "rs1",  "host" : "rs1/mongod1.replicaset.com:27017,mongod2.replicaset.com:27017,mongod3.replicaset.com:27017" }
    {  "_id" : "shard0000",  "host" : "mongod1.sharding.com:27016" }
databases:
    {  "_id" : "admin",  "partitioned" : false,  "primary" : "config" }
    {  "_id" : "newdb",  "partitioned" : true,  "primary" : "shard0000" }
            newdb.test
                    shard key: { "_id" : "hashed" }
                    chunks:
                        rs1       2
                        shard0000     2
                    { "_id" : { "$minKey" : 1 } } -->> { "_id" : NumberLong("-4611686018427387902") } on : rs1 Timestamp(2, 2)
                    { "_id" : NumberLong("-4611686018427387902") } -->> { "_id" : NumberLong(0) } on : rs1 Timestamp(2, 3)
                    { "_id" : NumberLong(0) } -->> { "_id" : NumberLong("4611686018427387902") } on : shard0000 Timestamp(2, 4)
                    { "_id" : NumberLong("4611686018427387902") } -->> { "_id" : { "$maxKey" : 1 } } on : shard0000 Timestamp(2, 5)
```

In order to test the sharding feature, we will insert data into the test collection in newdb. As you know, the mongo shell is a JavaScript environment, and you can run the JavaScript codes in this environment.

Using the following function, we insert the number 10,000 into the newdb database and test collection:

```
for (var i = 1; i <= 10000; i++) {
    db.test.insert({
        data: i
    });
}
```

You can simply run the preceding code in the mongo shell, and as a result, you have 10,000, as data on the collection test. This is shown in the following screenshot:

```
mongos> for (var i = 1; i <= 10000; i++) db.test.insert( { data : i } )
WriteResult({ "nInserted" : 1 })
```

After adding data to the collection, you can check other shards to see data on them. The following screenshot shows the mongo shell for the rs1 replica set. This is shown in the following screenshot:

```
rs1:PRIMARY> show dbs
admin   (empty)
local   0.453GB
newdb   0.203GB
rsdb    0.203GB
rs1:PRIMARY> use newdb
switched to db newdb
rs1:PRIMARY> show collections
system.indexes
test
rs1:PRIMARY>
```

As you can see, we created the database and collection on the mongos instance, but we have data on other shards too.

Because we have two shards at the moment, MongoDB splits data into two shards. So, if we run the following command to get the data count in a replica set, we will see fewer counts than what we inserted using the JavaScript code (10,000 items). The following code depicts this:

```
db.test.find().count()
```

The following screenshot shows the output of the preceding command:

```
rs1:PRIMARY> db.test.find().count()
5073
rs1:PRIMARY>
```

Interesting! We have 5,073 item counts in the replica set. If we get the same query from a standalone `mongod` instance, you can see the rest of the data in this shard as shown in the following screenshot:

```
> show dbs
admin    (empty)
local    (empty)
newdb    0.203125GB
> use newdb
switched to db newdb
> db.test.find().count()
4927
>
```

Well, the sharding feature distributes the entire dataset into two separate shards using our hash-based shard key.

Using the same method, you can define other shard keys, and MongoDB will use those shard keys to split data.

The following is another example of adding a shard key. In this example, we use shard keys x and y on collection test2. The command for this shard key is like the following:

```
sh.shardCollection("newdb.test2", { "x": 1, "y": 1 })
```

The result of issuing the preceding command is demonstrated in the following screenshot:

```
mongos> sh.shardCollection("newdb.test2", { "x": 1, "y": 1 } )
{ "collectionsharded" : "newdb.test2", "ok" : 1 }
```

Using this key, MongoDB splits data with the x field, and then if the collection has the same data on the x key, it will use the y field to split the data.

This screenshot illustrates the output of the `sh.status()` command after adding a new collection to a shard:

```
shards:
    {  "_id" : "rs1", "host" : "rs1/mongod1.replicaset.com:27017,mongod2.replicaset.com:27017,mongod3.replicaset.com:27017" }
    {  "_id" : "shard0000", "host" : "mongod1.sharding.com:27016" }
databases:
    {  "_id" : "admin", "partitioned" : false, "primary" : "config" }
    {  "_id" : "newdb", "partitioned" : true, "primary" : "shard0000" }
        newdb.test
            shard key: { "_id" : "hashed" }
            chunks:
                rs1        2
                shard0000  2
            {  "_id" : { "$minKey" : 1 } } -->> { "_id" : NumberLong("-4611686018427387902") } on : rs1 Timestamp(2, 2)
            {  "_id" : NumberLong("-4611686018427387902") } -->> { "_id" : NumberLong(0) } on : rs1 Timestamp(2, 3)
            {  "_id" : NumberLong(0) } -->> { "_id" : NumberLong("4611686018427387902") } on : shard0000 Timestamp(2, 4)
            {  "_id" : NumberLong("4611686018427387902") } -->> { "_id" : { "$maxKey" : 1 } } on : shard0000 Timestamp(2, 5)
        newdb.test2
            shard key: { "x" : 1, "y" : 1 }
            chunks:
                shard0000  1
            {  "x" : { "$minKey" : 1 }, "y" : { "$minKey" : 1 } } -->> { "x" : { "$maxKey" : 1 }, "y" : { "$maxKey" : 1 } } on : shard0000 Time
tamp(1, 0)
    {  "_id" : "rsdb", "partitioned" : false, "primary" : "rs1" }
    {  "_id" : "test_db", "partitioned" : false, "primary" : "shard0000" }
```

Now, we have two collections for sharding with two different sharding keys. After adding data, MongoDB splits data into different chunks and shards.

> In order to choose a good sharding key, there are several parameters that are important to consider. For more information on tips and hacks to choose a correct sharding key, please visit http://docs.mongodb.org/manual/tutorial/choose-a-shard-key/.

Summary

In this chapter, you learned how to enable the sharding feature for a MongoDB database. First of all, we prepared the environment and configured the hostnames for configuration servers. Then, you learned how to start a configuration server and establish a configuration server on a machine. You are recommended to host the configuration server on separate machines in a production environment, but for development, you can host them on a single machine.

After establishing the configuration servers, we added shards to sharding. For production uses, it's better to use a replica set for each shard, but for development and testing environments, we can host standalone mongod instances. For our example, we added two shards, one replica set, and a standalone mongod instance.

Also, you learned how to manage and control mongos instances using the mongo shell.

At the end, we created a database and collection to test the sharding feature on. You learned that we should enable sharding for the database first, then using the mongo shell, we enabled sharding for each collection using shard keys. Using JavaScript codes and a for-loop, we added some test data into the collection.

After adding data to the collection by using a query from the available shards, replica set, and standalone MongoDB instance, we learned that MongoDB splits data between available chunks using a defined shard key.

In the next chapter, you will learn how to improve the response time of the server using the methods that we learned in the previous chapters.

8
Analyzing and Improving Database Performance

After learning replication, sharding, and clustering solutions in MongoDB, in this chapter, we will review the possible ways and methods to improve the response time and performance of read/write operations. Improving the performance of the database depends on several parameters, so it's difficult to pack everything in a single chapter. Nevertheless, we will discuss topics related to performance improvement one by one.

Understanding profiling

To deal with poor performance in an application, we need a tool to find the problems and address the issues. In this chapter, we will focus on profiling, which is a popular method to debug and find the areas that affect performance in a program.

> In software engineering, profiling (**program profiling** and **software profiling**) is a form of dynamic program analysis that measures, for example, space (memory) or time, the complexity of a program, the use of particular instructions, or the frequency and duration of function calls. The most common use of profiling information is to aid program optimization. For more information, please visit http://en.wikipedia.org/wiki/Profiling_(computer_programming).

In the next sections, you will learn the basic considerations and configurations to enable and use the profiling facility in MongoDB.

Utilizing profiling

Writing an optimized query is one of the most significant factors to maximize performance in a database engine. When you are faced with performance issues, there is a method to find and fix the corresponding part or query. Profiling the database and queries is a method known to programmers to find bottlenecks and fix performance problems.

The good news is that MongoDB supports profiling for each instance or for each database. Using this feature, you can find the slowest queries in the program and address the issues by replacing the old queries with optimized versions.

MongoDB has a profiler engine that collects corresponding data for read/write operations, cursors, and database commands on a `mongod` process. The profiler engine is configurable for an instance or a database. Moreover, identical to all profiling methods, the profiler level is also configurable in three different levels. Each level is designed for a specific approach and the profiler engine works differently on each level.

After enabling and configuring the profiler engine, the MongoDB profiler engine collects all data in the `system.profile` collection. This collection contains documents that represent the profiler engine's output. The profiler engine supports different levels of profiling, so you can configure it to be correct based on your usage.

The following list shows the different levels of profiling available in MongoDB:

- **Level 0**: This means the profiler engine is turned off.

  The profiler engine won't log anything in this level. This is the default level for the profiler.

- **Level 1**: The profiler collects data under certain conditions.

  For instance, the profiler collects data for slow operations. By default, the profiler logs the queries slower than 100 milliseconds. However, you can change this setting using the `slowOpThresholdMs` option.

- **Level 2**: This means that the profiler engine collects data about all the operations in a database.

The profiler engine uses the `operationProfiling.slowOpThresholdMs` option to consider an operation as a slow operation. The default value for this option is 100 ms, but you can simply change it by configuring the option with another value in the `mongod` configuration file.

On the other hand, the second parameter of the `setProfilingLevel` function accepts the value for the `slowOpThresholdMs` option and overrides the default value (100 ms) with the given value.

In the next section, we will enable and configure the profiler for a database or `mongod` instance.

Enabling and configuring the profiler

To enable, configure, and use the profiler engine, open a `mongo` shell interface. Using this environment, you can enable the profiler engine or even get the profiler log from the database.

The structure of the `setProfilingLevel` function is as follows:

```
db.setProfilingLevel(level, slowms)
```

The first parameter is the level of the profiler, which is a mandatory parameter. The second and optional parameter, `slowms`, is the threshold in milliseconds to consider an operation as a slow operation.

In order to enable the profiler for a single database, you can simply use the following command in the `mongo` shell interface:

```
db.setProfilingLevel(2)
```

For instance, the preceding command enables the profiler and sets the profiler verbosity to the highest level. The profiler will collect all operation logs and save them in the `system.profile` collection.

It is worth mentioning that by using the following command, you can set both the level and the `slowOpThresholdMs` option at the same time for a database:

```
db.setProfilingLevel(1, 50)
```

The preceding command sets the profiling level to 1 and configures the `slowOpThresholdMs` option to 50 ms.

To disable the profiler engine, use following command:

```
db.setProfilingLevel(0)
```

To get the current profiler status, you can use the following command in the `mongo` shell:

```
db.getProfilingStatus()
```

The output of the preceding command should look like the following screenshot:

```
> db.getProfilingStatus()
{ "was" : 1, "slowms" : 10 }
>
```

The preceding command returns the current profiler level in the was field and the slowOpThresholdMs value using the slowms field.

Using the profiler log

1. In order to demonstrate the efficiency of the profiler engine, assume you have a database with a collection. This collection contains 100,000 records with the following schema:

    ```
    {
        "_id": ObjectId("533b1f9ae4671f0000000004"),
        "x": "1"
    }
    ```

2. Then, using the setProfilingLevel function, we enable the profiler for the database as shown in the following screenshot:

    ```
    > db.setProfilingLevel(1, 10)
    { "was" : 1, "slowms" : 10, "ok" : 1 }
    >
    ```

3. For this example, we use 10 for the second parameter of the setProfilingLevel function, which defines the slow operation threshold in milliseconds.

    To produce an operation with a slow execution time, we can query testcollection and sort all the results descending till field x. This is shown in the following screenshot:

```
> db.testcollection.find().sort({x: -1})
{ "_id" : ObjectId("536eee4c330df062eeca0eeb"), "x" : 99999 }
{ "_id" : ObjectId("536eee4c330df062eeca0eea"), "x" : 99998 }
{ "_id" : ObjectId("536eee4c330df062eeca0ee9"), "x" : 99997 }
{ "_id" : ObjectId("536eee4c330df062eeca0ee8"), "x" : 99996 }
{ "_id" : ObjectId("536eee4c330df062eeca0ee7"), "x" : 99995 }
{ "_id" : ObjectId("536eee4c330df062eeca0ee6"), "x" : 99994 }
{ "_id" : ObjectId("536eee4c330df062eeca0ee5"), "x" : 99993 }
{ "_id" : ObjectId("536eee4c330df062eeca0ee4"), "x" : 99992 }
{ "_id" : ObjectId("536eee4c330df062eeca0ee3"), "x" : 99991 }
{ "_id" : ObjectId("536eee4c330df062eeca0ee2"), "x" : 99990 }
{ "_id" : ObjectId("536eee4c330df062eeca0ee1"), "x" : 99989 }
{ "_id" : ObjectId("536eee4c330df062eeca0ee0"), "x" : 99988 }
{ "_id" : ObjectId("536eee4c330df062eeca0edf"), "x" : 99987 }
{ "_id" : ObjectId("536eee4c330df062eeca0ede"), "x" : 99986 }
{ "_id" : ObjectId("536eee4c330df062eeca0edd"), "x" : 99985 }
{ "_id" : ObjectId("536eee4c330df062eeca0edc"), "x" : 99984 }
{ "_id" : ObjectId("536eee4c330df062eeca0edb"), "x" : 99983 }
{ "_id" : ObjectId("536eee4c330df062eeca0eda"), "x" : 99982 }
{ "_id" : ObjectId("536eee4c330df062eeca0ed9"), "x" : 99981 }
{ "_id" : ObjectId("536eee4c330df062eeca0ed8"), "x" : 99980 }
Type "it" for more
>
```

4. After executing the operation using the `mongo` shell interface, you can fetch logs from the profiler collection. Fetching profiler logs is as easy as issuing this command in the `mongo` shell:

```
db.system.profile.find()
```

5. After issuing the preceding command, the output of the profiler will be as follows:

```
{
    "op": "query",
    "ns": "testdb.testcollection",
    "query": {
        "query": {

        },
        "orderby": {
            "x": 1
        }
    },
    "cursorid": 379565678896,
    "ntoreturn": 0,
    "ntoskip": 0,
    "nscanned": 100000,
    "nscannedObjects": 100000,
    "scanAndOrder": true,
    "keyUpdates": 0,
```

```
    "numYield": 0,
    "lockStats": {
        "timeLockedMicros": {
            "r": NumberLong(424880),
            "w": NumberLong(0)
        },
        "timeAcquiringMicros": {
            "r": NumberLong(4),
            "w": NumberLong(3)
        }
    },
    "nreturned": 101,
    "responseLength": 3353,
    "millis": 424,
    "execStats": {
        "type": "SORT",
        "works": 100104,
        "yields": 782,
        "unyields": 782,
        "invalidates": 0,
        "advanced": 101,
        "needTime": 100002,
        "needFetch": 0,
        "isEOF": 0,
        "forcedFetches": 0,
        "memUsage": 4100000,
        "memLimit": 33554432,
        "children": [{
            "type": "COLLSCAN",
            "works": 100002,
            "yields": 782,
            "unyields": 782,
            "invalidates": 0,
            "advanced": 100000,
            "needTime": 1,
            "needFetch": 0,
            "isEOF": 1,
            "docsTested": 100000,
            "children": []
        }]
    },
    "ts": ISODate("2014-05-11T03:30:17.645Z"),
    "client": "127.0.0.1",
    "allUsers": [],
```

```
        "user": ""
    }
```

As you can observe in the preceding output, there are a lot of fields in the profiler log, but we will only review some of the important fields:

- `ts`: This field shows the operation's timestamp, for example, `ISODate ("2014-05-11T03:30:17.645Z")`.

- `op`: This field is used to detect the type of the operation.

  The possible values are:

  ○ `insert`

  ○ `query`

  ○ `update`

  ○ `remove`

  ○ `getmore`

  ○ `command`

- `ns`: This is the target namespace of the executed operation. This is a string starting with a database, followed by a dot and the collection name, for example, `testdb.testcollection`.

- `query`: This field is a detailed plan of the operation's query. The following is an example of this field:

```
"query": {
    "query": {

    },
    "orderby": {
        "x": 1
    }
}
```

 Profiler output contains more fields. To get more information about all the fields, please visit `http://docs.mongodb.org/manual/ reference/database-profiler/`.

Using the database profiler engine, you can catch slow operations and find a detailed explanation of each one to help you patch them.

Introducing other analytics methods

MongoDB provides the `explain()` function, which provides you a detailed procedure for the current operator. For instance, consider following command:

```
db.testcollection.find().sort({x: -1}).explain()
```

The preceding command will execute the `find` operator and sort the records descending from the x field. Then, the `explain()` function shows an output as follows:

```
{
    "cursor": "BasicCursor",
    "isMultiKey": false,
    "n": 100000,
    "nscannedObjects": 100000,
    "nscanned": 100000,
    "nscannedObjectsAllPlans": 100000,
    "nscannedAllPlans": 100000,
    "scanAndOrder": true,
    "indexOnly": false,
    "nYields": 1563,
    "nChunkSkips": 0,
    "millis": 406,
    "server": "mongotest:27017",
    "filterSet": false
}
```

In the preceding JSON format, the n field is an integer that reflects the number of affected records. Also, the `indexOnly` field is Boolean and returns `true` only when returned fields are already indexed.

Moreover, the `millis` field is an integer value that shows the time spent in milliseconds to complete the operator.

 In order to find more information about the `explain()` function, please visit `http://docs.mongodb.org/manual/reference/method/cursor.explain/`.

Furthermore, MongoDB provides a great facility for developers to get a report from the current running operations. The `db.currentOp()` function can be used to get this report from a database engine.

This function accepts one optional parameter. The general format of using this function is as follows:

db.currentOp(true)

You can use this function without any parameter or pass a Boolean value for the first parameter, that is, enable the verbosity mode of a function.

The following JSON format shows one record of this function:

```
{
    "opid": 2580,
    "active": true,
    "op": "query",
    "ns": "testdb.testcollection",
    "query": {
        "$query": {
            "$or": [{
                "name": "boo"
            }],
            "isActive": true,
            "type": "1"
        },
        "orderby": {
            "creationDate": -1
        }
    },
    "client": "127.0.0.1:60371",
    "desc": "conn613",
    "threadId": "0x13d510000",
    "connectionId": 613,
    "waitingForLock": false,
    "numYields": 0,
    "lockStats": {
        "timeLockedMicros": {
            "r": NumberLong(203),
            "w": NumberLong(0)
        },
        "timeAcquiringMicros": {
            "r": NumberLong(4),
            "w": NumberLong(0)
        }
    }
}
```

The same as in the previous profiling functions, the preceding log provides some explanations about the in-progress operations such as opid, ns, or query. The opid field shows the process ID, which can be used as a process ID parameter to kill the operation using the db.killOp() function.

Identical to the previous log formats, the ns field shows the namespace of the operation. The query field reflects the query parameters and functions, which can be used to get information about operation conditions and settings.

> For more information about the db.currentOp() function, refer to the documentation page at http://docs.mongodb.org/manual/reference/method/db.currentOp/.

Introducing indexes

In order to boost the database's performance, we can use indexes to categorize the records of a collection. Thus, the database engine can perform read/write queries faster than before.

> Indexes support the efficient execution of queries in MongoDB. Without indexes, MongoDB must scan every document in a collection to select those documents that match the query statement. These collection scans are inefficient because they require mongod to process a larger volume of data than an index for each operation. For more information on indexes, please visit http://docs.mongodb.org/manual/core/indexes-introduction/.

If you frequently work with specific fields in a collection, we recommend that you define an index for them to improve performance. For instance, if you sort a collection based on certain fields regularly, you can make that field an indexed field so that the database engine can perform the query much faster.

To define an index for a specific field, you can use following command:

```
db.news.ensureIndex({ title: 1 })
```

The preceding command creates an index for the title field of the news collection. After creating the index field, if you issue the following command, you will get the result faster than before:

```
db.news.find().sort({ title: -1 })
```

It doesn't matter if you sort the document's field in the ascending or descending order because the database engine can read the index in both directions. It is worth mentioning that it's impossible to tell you everything about index features in one section. So, for more information on the concept of indexes and tutorials, please visit `http://docs.mongodb.org/manual/indexes/`.

Using projection

Another approach to perform faster queries in MongoDB is to use the projection feature. With projection, you limit the output of the database to specific fields and remove the redundant data from the result. Thus, the output of the database engine will be smaller and the client can fetch and download the result faster than before.

The use of the projection feature is as easy as passing a collection to the second parameter of the `find` method, which is similar to the following command:

```
db.testcollection.find({}, {_id: 0})
```

For instance, in the preceding command, the engine returns all documents but it excludes the _id field.

The same as in the previous example, the following command returns records with a value greater than 500 for the field x. All the records contain only the field x as shown in the following command line:

```
db.testcollection.find({ x: {$gt: 500} }, {x: 1, _id:0})
```

It is worth mentioning that passing the value 0 to the projection option excludes the field from the final result and passing 1 includes it.

Limiting the number of records returned

Another trick to improve the performance of the `find` operations is limiting the output records to specific numbers of items. Thus, the engine only returns a subset of all records and a client downloads a smaller piece of data. Both of these methods together can boost the overall performance of an operation.

To limit the output to smaller items, you can use the `limit()` function, similar to the following function:

```
db.testcollection.find().limit(2)
```

In the preceding example, the database engine returns only two records from all the inserted records based on the given sort options.

Reviewing the hardware considerations

Changing a machine's hardware to increase the performance of a database is a common pattern among database administrators. As discussed in the previous chapters, MongoDB is designed for horizontal scaling, but some considerations about a machine's hardware configurations can help the database engine work smoothly.

Using an SSD hard drive can improve the database engine's performance significantly. Because MongoDB uses disk I/O to access data and it happens randomly, with an SSD hard drive, the database engine can read/write data faster from the disk, so the overall performance will be better.

For mongod instances, make sure that the machine has sufficient RAM. Also, since the mongod instance stores data in RAM to access the database faster, it's important to have enough RAM capacity. If you don't have enough RAM on a single server, use clustering solutions to use the RAM capacity of all the machines.

We recommend that you use each machine for a single role, meaning it would be better if each mongod instance is hosted on a separate machine. However, for arbiters and query routers, you can use a single server. But because the mongod instances perform a significant task, using separate machines for each one can impact the performance.

Furthermore, as discussed in *Chapter 6*, *Understanding the Concept of Sharding*, and *Chapter 7*, *Sharding in Action*, using multiple query routers can balance the requests between different machines and, finally, the entire database performance gets better. To shard networks and in a production environment, you should use replica sets instead of single mongod instances.

Summary

In this chapter, we reviewed basic approaches to profiling, analyzed the database engine, and you learned how to boost the performance of a database. First, we introduced the profiling feature, which is a method to analyze and find slow operations in a database. Then, you learned how to enable and use profiler logs in MongoDB to find slow operations. Next, you learned other profiling functions and methods to find the in-progress operations in MongoDB or get a report from a specific query. Furthermore, we reviewed an example of using profiling for slow operations and how to find them in the system.profile collection.

Next, you discovered how to use indexing, projection, and limiting features to limit the database output to a specific subset of data and perform operations faster than before. Also, we demonstrated an example of indexing, projection, and limiting features.

At the end of chapter, we reviewed some hardware considerations that can be used to boost the overall performance of the database engine. Although MongoDB is designed for horizontal scaling, rather than vertical scaling, these considerations can help administrators improve the performance of a database engine.

9

Migrating Instances and Reducing Downtime

Migrating a MongoDB instance to another machine is a common situation that you might face. This migration could be used to upgrade the server or move the instance to another data center. In the production environment, it's important to avoid downtime while moving the database to another machine.

The common method to move the instance is installing the database engine on the new server, copying the database path from an existing server, pasting it into the new server, and then starting a new instance. This method has some problems, as you should disable writing while moving database logs to the new server. In this chapter, we will introduce a way to move the entire database from an existing server to another server with no downtime.

Understanding the migration process

As you already learned in previous chapters, there are two main ways to deploy a MongoDB instance: using replica sets for deployment in a production environment and using a single mongod instance for development or testing.

Although it's not a good idea to use a single mongod instance for the production environment, we will introduce both methods to move a single mongod instance and replica set.

First of all, there is a simple hack to migrate a replica set to another server. As you know, if you add a new member to an existing replica set, this member will synchronize its `oplog` with the current `primary` node. This is shown in the following diagram:

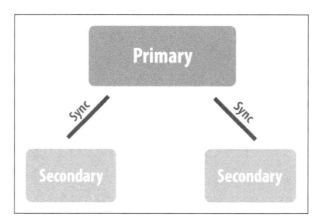

Let's assume we have a `primary` node in our existing server, then we add a new node to the existing replica set. Obviously, initially it will be a `secondary` node. This `secondary` node is empty, but it synchronizes its `oplog` with the primary server inside the existing server. This depends on the amount of data on the existing server, the network connection, and the hardware configurations.

To migrate a single `mongod` instance, there are different ways, but all of them have at least a brief outage. Generally, the procedure to move the standalone `mongod` instance is as follows:

1. Stop the existing node.
2. Copy the data to a new server.
3. Start a new node.
4. Point applications to a new address.

The following diagram illustrates this procedure:

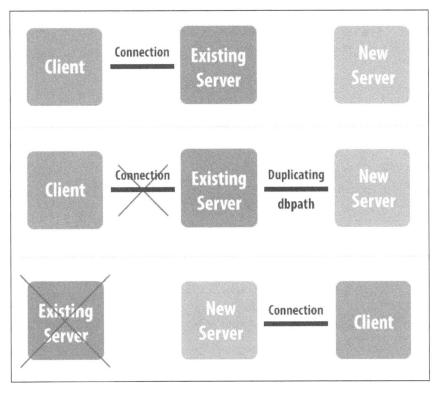

However, there is another, and better way to the preceding scenario: convert the existing standalone mongod instance to a replica set and follow the same method to migrate replica sets.

Migrating a replica set in action

For the first part of the migration, we are going to migrate a replica set. In this section, we will learn how to add a new node to the replica set and wait for the synchronization process. Then, we remove the old node and make sure that the migration has been completed successfully.

Explaining the migration process

In this scenario, we have a replica set with one `primary`, one `secondary`, and one `arbiter` node. The following diagram shows the replica set and its members:

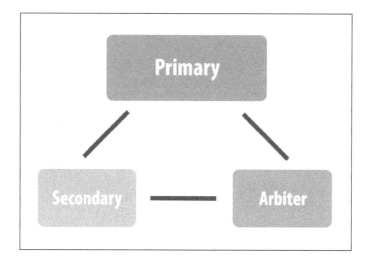

Then, we will add a new node to the existing replica set and remove the current `primary` node.

In this part, a new `secondary` node synchronizes its `oplog` with the `primary` node in a background process. After completing synchronization, you can safely remove the `primary` node and wait for the replica set to choose the new `primary` node. This is the election phase.

The following diagram shows the election procedure:

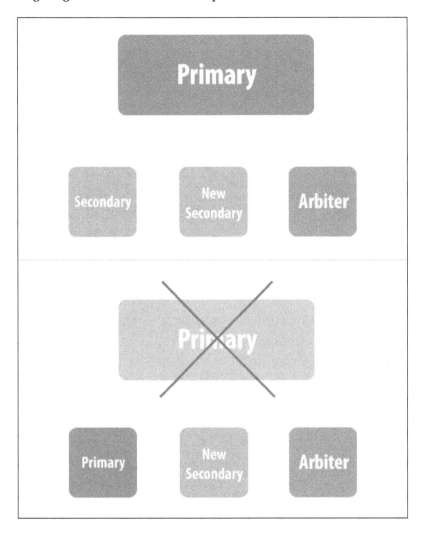

The current replica set has three members. These include one `primary` node, one `secondary` node, and an `arbiter` node. The following screenshot shows the current status of our replica set:

```
{
        "set" : "rs1",
        "date" : ISODate("2014-05-27T14:13:35Z"),
        "myState" : 1,
        "members" : [
                {
                        "_id" : 0,
                        "name" : "mongod1.replicaset.com:27017",
                        "health" : 1,
                        "state" : 1,
                        "stateStr" : "PRIMARY",
                        "uptime" : 329,
                        "optime" : Timestamp(1401199999, 1),
                        "optimeDate" : ISODate("2014-05-27T14:13:19Z"),
                        "electionTime" : Timestamp(1401199798, 1),
                        "electionDate" : ISODate("2014-05-27T14:09:58Z"),
                        "self" : true
                },
                {
                        "_id" : 2,
                        "name" : "mongod3.replicaset.com:27017",
                        "health" : 1,
                        "state" : 2,
                        "stateStr" : "SECONDARY",
                        "uptime" : 16,
                        "optime" : Timestamp(1401199999, 1),
                        "optimeDate" : ISODate("2014-05-27T14:13:19Z"),
                        "lastHeartbeat" : ISODate("2014-05-27T14:13:33Z"),
                        "lastHeartbeatRecv" : ISODate("2014-05-27T14:13:34Z"),
                        "pingMs" : 7,
                        "lastHeartbeatMessage" : "syncing to: mongod1.replicaset.com:27017",
                        "syncingTo" : "mongod1.replicaset.com:27017"
                },
                {
                        "_id" : 3,
                        "name" : "arbiter1.replicaset.com:20000",
                        "health" : 1,
                        "state" : 7,
                        "stateStr" : "ARBITER",
                        "uptime" : 16,
                        "lastHeartbeat" : ISODate("2014-05-27T14:13:33Z"),
                        "lastHeartbeatRecv" : ISODate("2014-05-27T14:13:33Z"),
                        "pingMs" : 0
                }
        ],
        "ok" : 1
}
rs1:PRIMARY>
```

Suppose we want to migrate a database from a `mongod1.replicaset.com` hostname to a new Ubuntu machine where the server's hostname is `mongod2.replicaset.com`.

The next sections of this chapter will show you the process of adding a new server and syncing data from an existing server to a new server.

Adding a new machine

In this section, we will add our new machine to the existing replica set. The hostname of the new node is `mongod2.replicaset.com`.

Using the `rs.add()` function, we will add the new node to the existing replica set as shown in the following screenshot:

```
rs1:PRIMARY> rs.add("mongod2.replicaset.com:27017")
{ "ok" : 1 }
```

The following screenshot shows the status of the replica set after adding the new node:

```
{
    "_id" : 4,
    "name" : "mongod2.replicaset.com:27017",
    "health" : 1,
    "state" : 6,
    "stateStr" : "UNKNOWN",
    "uptime" : 5,
    "optime" : Timestamp(0, 0),
    "optimeDate" : ISODate("1970-01-01T00:00:00Z"),
    "lastHeartbeat" : ISODate("2014-05-27T14:52:35Z"),
    "lastHeartbeatRecv" : ISODate("1970-01-01T00:00:00Z"),
    "pingMs" : 0,
    "lastHeartbeatMessage" : "still initializing"
}
```

The replica set members can have different statuses. You can check the status of a member using the `state` and `stateStr` fields. The state field shows the status of a member using an integer value and the `stateStr` field shows the status label.

As you can see, after adding the new node to the existing replica set, the new node's status is UNKNOWN. This is because it is in the initialization phase.

You should wait a while and let the new member communicate with the `primary` node, and then get the configurations for the replica set and the members relationship. The next state for the member will be SECONDARY and `state ID` is 2.

 You can read more about replica set member's statuses at http://docs.mongodb.org/manual/reference/replica-states/.

The following screenshot shows the status of a member after completing the synchronization process:

```
{
        "_id" : 4,
        "name" : "mongod2.replicaset.com:27017",
        "health" : 1,
        "state" : 2,
        "stateStr" : "SECONDARY",
        "uptime" : 457,
        "optime" : Timestamp(1401202353, 1),
        "optimeDate" : ISODate("2014-05-27T14:52:33Z"),
        "lastHeartbeat" : ISODate("2014-05-27T15:00:09Z"),
        "lastHeartbeatRecv" : ISODate("2014-05-27T15:00:09Z"),
        "pingMs" : 0,
        "syncingTo" : "mongod1.replicaset.com:27017"
}
```

This status shows that the new member is ready to use. Now, we can disconnect the current primary node and let the replica set choose the new primary node. Please note that clients can perform write operations on the primary node. Thus, if we disconnect the current primary node and wait for the replica set to choose the new primary member, clients cannot perform write operations.

This problem can happen to read operations, but you can simply allow clients to read from the secondary members. However, you can't set this option for write operations.

Understanding replica set election problems

In a replica set, only the primary node can accept write operations. By default, clients perform read operations from the primary node too. However, you can change this condition for a read operation and route the client's read requests to the secondary nodes.

Suppose we have the testcollection collection and we want to read data with mongo shell. At the first attempt, you will face with an error as shown in the following screenshot:

```
rs1:SECONDARY> db.testcoll.find()
error: { "$err" : "not master and slaveOk=false", "code" : 13435 }
rs1:SECONDARY>
```

Then, you can allow this node to be readable from clients using the following command:

```
rs.slaveOk(true)
```

The following screenshot shows the output after using the preceding command:

```
rs1:SECONDARY> rs.slaveOk(true)
rs1:SECONDARY> db.testcoll.find()
{ "_id" : ObjectId("53862800397828c37c72704d"), "a" : 1 }
rs1:SECONDARY>
```

It's recommended that you enable read operations for secondary members. Using this approach, you can route read operations for secondary members. Thus, clients can perform read operations even if the primary node is not available.

Now, we don't have any issues with read operations while election, but the write operations still won't execute. This is because the primary node is not accessible. This is the only part that the MongoDB replica set doesn't handle.

There is a simple hack to avoid errors and perform write operations after the election process. You can use a queuing module in your programming language to put write operations in a queue if they are faced with an error, and you can try to write operation them in an interval. With this approach, not only you can fix the issue with the election process, but you can also provide a highly available application.

The following diagram shows this queue and relations between clients and the MongoDB engine:

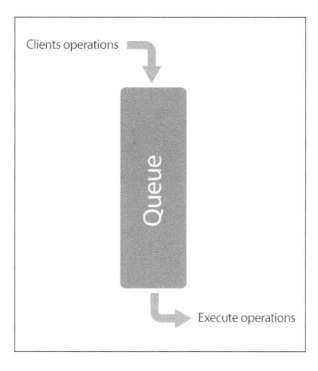

Removing the existing machine

At this step, we are going to remove or disable the current `primary` node from the replica set and let the cluster choose the new member. After removing the `primary` node, the replica set selects another `primary` node and changes the nodes' relationship.

The following screenshot shows the status of the old `primary` node after it is disabled:

```
{
    "_id" : 0,
    "name" : "mongod1.replicaset.com:27017",
    "health" : 0,
    "state" : 8,
    "stateStr" : "(not reachable/healthy)",
    "uptime" : 0,
    "optime" : Timestamp(1401300994, 1),
    "optimeDate" : ISODate("2014-05-28T18:16:34Z"),
    "lastHeartbeat" : ISODate("2014-05-28T15:18:46Z"),
    "lastHeartbeatRecv" : ISODate("2014-05-28T15:18:25Z"),
    "pingMs" : 0,
    "syncingTo" : "mongod2.replicaset.com:27017"
```

As you can see, the status of this node is `8`, which means it's not reachable.

Furthermore, the following screenshot illustrates the status of the new member that became a `primary` node after election:

```
{
    "_id" : 4,
    "name" : "mongod2.replicaset.com:27017",
    "health" : 1,
    "state" : 1,
    "stateStr" : "PRIMARY",
    "uptime" : 4058975,
    "optime" : Timestamp(1401300994, 1),
    "optimeDate" : ISODate("2014-05-28T18:16:34Z"),
    "self" : true
}
```

Now, using a `mongo` shell in the `primary` node, you can remove the old server from the replica set:

```
rs.remove("mongod1.replicaset.com:27017")
```

Using this method and replication, we moved the database from an old machine to the new server. This procedure can be used for other nodes, but make sure that you have an odd number of members; otherwise, you will face issues during election.

Using an arbiter member enables you to have even number of members in a replica set, since the arbiter can vote in the election process.

Migrating a standalone mongod instance

Basically, there are two ways to move a standalone mongod instance to another server:

- Convert it to a replica set and follow replica set migration
- Move dbpath to the new server manually

However, the first approach is recommended since it has less outage. We will introduce both methods in further sections.

Converting an existing instance to a replica set

There are some straightforward steps to convert a standalone instance to a replica set. As you already learned in previous chapters, a replica set should have a name. This name is configurable via a configuration file or command-line parameters for the mongod process.

In order to define the replica set's name, you can use the replSet setting. For instance, the following configuration file sets the replica set name to rs1:

```
logpath = /var/log/mongodb.log
port = 27017
fork = true
replSet = rs1
```

Also, you can use the following command-line parameters:

mongod --port 27017 --dbpath /var/log/mongodb.log --replSet rs1

In order to set the name for the replica set, you should shut down the mongod instance and restart it with a new configuration file (or command-line parameters). At this step, you have a brief outage since you have to shut down the mongod instance.

After restarting the mongod instance, you should connect to the mongod instance using the mongo interactive shell and issue the following command:

rs.initiate()

After issuing the preceding command, the replica set is ready. Use the `rs.status()` to check the status of the replica set.

For the rest of migration process, we will follow the same method that we followed to migrate replica sets. You can add the new node (the new server) and after completing synchronization, remove the current node from the replica set.

> Make sure that you have an odd number of members in your replica set in all the steps you perform.

Moving dbpath to the new server

MongoDB uses a directory called `dbpath` to store everything related to the instance, including databases, collections, users, and so on.

A very simple but error-prone way to migrate the `mongod` instance is to copy this directory to the new server and start the new instance using this existing directory.

The following screenshot shows the content of a database directory:

```
→ mongodb4 l
total 1114120
drwxrwxrwx  10 root  wheel   340B May 28 23:14 .
drwxr-xr-x  13 root  wheel   442B May 27 18:28 ..
drwxr-xr-x   3 root  wheel   102B May 28 23:14 journal
-rw-------   4 root  wheel    64M May 27 18:39 local.0
-rw-------   4 root  wheel   128M May 27 18:39 local.1
-rw-------   3 root  wheel   256M May 28 23:15 local.2
-rw-------   1 root  wheel    16M May 28 23:15 local.ns
-rwxr-xr-x   1 root  wheel     5B May 28 23:14 mongod.lock
-rw-------   1 root  wheel    64M May 28 22:47 test.0
-rw-------   1 root  wheel    16M May 28 22:47 test.ns
→ mongodb4
```

You can use `dbpath` to define the directory path for an instance. The following configuration file sets the database directory to /db/mongodb:

```
dbpath = /db/mongodb
port = 27017
```

Also, you can use the following command-line parameter:

```
mongod --port 27017 --dbpath /db/mongodb
```

After moving the database directory to the new server and configuring the `dbpath`, you can start a new instance in the new server and point the application's database connection to the new sever.

Summary

In this chapter, you learned how to move a MongoDB instance to a new server without downtime. First of all, you learned that the standalone mongod instance is not highly available. So, while migrating, you might be faced with a brief outage.

In the first part of this chapter, you learned how to migrate a replica set using the replication feature of MongoDB. This approach has no downtime and is simple and straightforward since replication moves the database completely.

Also, you learned that the only concern for this method is that clients cannot perform write operations during election, and we introduced a hack to perform these operations at an interval. Meanwhile, we learned how to route read operations during election using the slaveOk function.

Then, you learned how to convert a standalone mongod instance to a replica set and follow the same approach to migrate a replica set for the standalone instance. Furthermore, we introduced a way to move the database by duplicating the dbpath and pointing the new instance to the existing database directory.

In the next chapter, we will talk about monitoring and diagnosing the MongoDB instance using different built-in and third-party tools.

10
Monitoring and Troubleshooting the Database

This is our last chapter. Here, you will learn how to manage and control the MongoDB instances, including replica sets, shards, and standalone mongod instances. We will review monitoring, profiling, and reporting utilities in MongoDB. Also, we will study the diagnostic strategies that help database administrators prevent database engine failures. Step-by-step, we will learn how to work with these utilities.

Understanding monitoring strategies

Monitoring is one of the critical tasks of database administration. Using correct monitoring tools based on the situation and context can help database administrators to provide a readily-available database engine. For instance, by configuring the correct alert messages in database high overload, the database administrator can follow an appropriate method to add a new node to the cluster or upgrade the existing server.

The good news is that MongoDB has many monitoring and profiling tools. In the previous chapters, we used some of these tools, such as profiling. In order to monitor the database, you can use different approaches based on your context. If you want to have a real-time report of a database or check the currently running tasks or read/write operations, you can use the built-in database commands or utilities.

On the other hand, in certain situations when you want to diagnose a database, you can simply use the profiling tools. These tools come in handy when you want to find slow operations in a highly overloaded database. Thus, you can find slow operations, fix them, and prevent the consumption of more resources.

Also, there are a lot of self-hosted and hosted SaaS tools that make database management much easier for the administrator. These tools are mostly web-based. You can connect your MongoDB instance to the utility and check the reports online by using your web browsers. Also, using some of the utilities, you can define an alert message based on certain conditions. The system will send you a message when all the conditions are correct via e-mail, text message, and so on. For instance, you can set up an alert message when the memory usage of a server is more than 90 percent.

The MongoDB instance emits useful logfiles according to the first startup parameters (verbose mode). Moreover, the database administrator can use these logfiles to realize the database engine situation.

The following diagram shows the different categories of database monitoring/diagnosing:

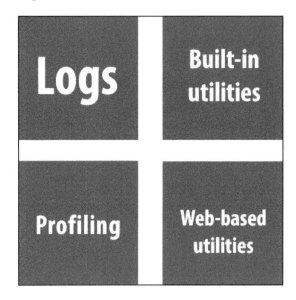

In the next sections, you will learn about all of the aforementioned categories in detail.

Utilizing the profiling feature

We already used the profiling feature in *Chapter 8, Analyzing and Improving Database Performance* to check a database and improve the performance of a database. As profiling is one of the diagnosing methods, we will take a quick look at this feature again in this chapter.

Profiling is a technique to detect slow operations. Thus, through it you can find inefficient operations and improve performance by altering operations and queries.

To enable profiling for a MongoDB instance, you can use following function:

```
db.setProfilingLevel(level, slowms)
```

The following table shows the parameters of the `setProfilingLevel` function:

Parameter	Description
level	This refers to verbosity level of profiling.
slowms	This is optional. It is used to define the slow operations threshold in milliseconds.

The following command is a sample of issuing the preceding function in the `mongo` interactive shell:

db.setProfilingLevel(1, 1000)

So, the preceding command enables profiling for the MongoDB instance with level 1 and threshold 1000 milliseconds.

The output of this command in the `mongo` shell is same as the following screenshot:

```
> db.setProfilingLevel(1, 1000)
{ "was" : 0, "slowms" : 100, "ok" : 1 }
>
```

The MongoDB engine supports three main levels of profiling. The following table shows the three different levels of profiling:

Level	Description
0	This indicates that profiling is disabled
1	This refers to only slow log operations
2	This refers to all log operations

When using the first level of profiling, the database's profiler doesn't save anything related to operations. With level 1, the profiler logs slow operations.

There is a setting parameter that defines the slow operations threshold. Using the `slowOpThresholdMs` configuration parameter, you can define a threshold for slow operations. Then, the profiler logs operations with slower execution time than the defined value.

To define the `slowOpThresholdMs` parameter, you can either use a configuration file to define the value or you can pass the value to the second parameter of the `setProfilingLevel` function, as explained earlier.

By using level 2 of profiling, the profiler records all operations without considering any conditions.

To understand the structure of this function better, consider the following command:

```
db.setProfilingLevel(1, 1000)
```

After issuing the preceding command, the database profiler records all operations with an execution time greater than 1000 milliseconds.

 Using the profiler negatively affects performance because the profiler records redundant data for a part, or the entire database operations. It's recommended to keep it off unless you need to diagnose the database.

After configuring the profiler engine, you can query logs from database using the `system.profile` collection.

The following screenshot illustrates the output of this query:

```
> db.system.profile.find().pretty()
{
        "op" : "query",
        "ns" : "test.system.profile",
        "query" : {

        },
        "ntoreturn" : 0,
        "ntoskip" : 0,
        "nscanned" : 0,
        "nscannedObjects" : 0,
        "keyUpdates" : 0,
        "numYield" : 0,
        "lockStats" : {
                        "timeLockedMicros" : {
                                "r" : NumberLong(93),
                                "w" : NumberLong(0)
                        },
                        "timeAcquiringMicros" : {
                                "r" : NumberLong(5),
                                "w" : NumberLong(5)
                        }
        },
        "nreturned" : 0,
        "responseLength" : 20,
        "millis" : 0,
        "execStats" : {
                        "type" : "COLLSCAN",
                        "works" : 2,
                        "yields" : 0,
                        "unyields" : 0,
                        "invalidates" : 0,
                        "advanced" : 0,
                        "needTime" : 1,
                        "needFetch" : 0,
                        "isEOF" : 1,
                        "docsTested" : 0,
                        "children" : [ ]
        },
        "ts" : ISODate("2014-05-21T17:58:24.616Z"),
        "client" : "127.0.0.1",
        "allUsers" : [ ],
        "user" : ""
}
```

The profiler engine logs operations with its related information. The document generated by profiler contains different fields, and you can read a complete manual about each field at `http://docs.mongodb.org/manual/reference/database-profiler/`.

In order to check the current status of profiler, you can use the following command:

`db.getProfilingStatus()`

The following screenshot shows the output of the preceding command:

```
> db.getProfilingStatus()
{ "was" : 2, "slowms" : 1000 }
>
```

 To read more about profiling and other related commands and techniques, please refer to `http://docs.mongodb.org/manual/tutorial/manage-the-database-profiler/`.

Utilizing the built-in reporting tools

MongoDB installs some built-in reporting and management tools while installing the database engine. These tools are useful to get a brief report from the database engine, such as operations that are currently running.

mongotop

The `mongotop` utility is a tool you can use to get real-time statistics of MongoDB.

This utility reports the current read/write operations of an available instance. The `mongotop` utility shows the report per database and collection so that you can track them easily.

In order to use this utility, you can issue the following command in the command-line interface:

`mongotop`

The following screenshot shows a simple output of this utility:

ns	total	read	write	2014-05-22T15:12:53
testdb.testcollection	773ms	773ms	0ms	
testdb.system.profile	0ms	0ms	0ms	
testdb.system.namespaces	0ms	0ms	0ms	
testdb.system.indexes	0ms	0ms	0ms	
test.system.profile	0ms	0ms	0ms	
test.system.namespaces	0ms	0ms	0ms	

The `mongotop` utility emits the report at a specified interval and refreshes the command-line environment automatically.

mongostat

The `mongostat` tool gives you a real-time report of the MongoDB performance statistics.

The `mongostat` tool is a useful to check the performance of a currently running MongoDB instance. It shows the count of operations per database with different types of operations such as query, insert, update, or delete.

To use this utility, issue the following command in the command-line interface:

```
mongostat
```

The following screenshot shows the output of this command:

```
➜  ~  mongostat
connected to: 127.0.0.1
insert query update delete getmore command flushes mapped  vsize   res locked % idx miss %     qr|qw   ar|aw netIn netOut conn     time
     0     0      0      0       0       1       0   160m  2.76g   53m      0          0         0|0     0|0   62b    1k    6  20:22:09
     0     3      0      0       0       1       0   160m  2.76g   53m      0          0         0|0     0|0  340b   46k    6  20:22:10
     0     5      0      0       0       1       0   160m  2.76g   53m      0          0         0|0     0|0  298b   31k    6  20:22:11
     0     2      0      0       0       1       0   160m  2.76g   53m      0          0         0|0     0|0  239b   12k    6  20:22:12
     0     9      0      0       0       1       0   160m  2.76g   53m      0          0         0|0     0|0  694b   82k    6  20:22:13
     0     1      0      0       0       1       0   160m  2.76g   53m      0          0         0|0     0|0  121b    6k    6  20:22:14
     0     0      0      0       0       1       0   160m  2.76g   53m      0          0         0|0     0|0   62b    1k    6  20:22:15
     0     0      0      0       0       1       0   160m  2.76g   53m      0          0         0|0     0|0   62b    1k    6  20:22:16
```

Enabling the web-based console

MongoDB provides a simple web-based interface, which you can use to get a brief report from the database engine. It shows the replica set's status, the client's statistics, and more.

To enable the web-based console, you should set the `httpInterface` configuration to `true`.

To enable the `http` console, you can use the following command:

```
mongod --httpinterface
```

After issuing the preceding command, the web-based console will be available on the `127.0.0.1` port; the port value is 1000 more than the configured `mongod` port.

The following screenshot shows an output of this console:

mongod mongotest

List all commands I Replica set status

Commands: buildInfo cursorInfo features hostInfo isMaster listDatabases replSetGetStatus serverStatus top

```
db version v2.6.0
git hash: nogitversion
sys info: Darwin minimavericks.local 13.1.0 Darwin Kernel Version 13.1.0: Thu Jan 16 19:40:37 PST 2014; root:xnu-2422.90.20~2/RE
uptime: 2 seconds
```

overview (only reported if can acquire read lock quickly)

```
time to get readlock: 0ms
# databases: 3
# Cursors: 0
replication:
master: 0
slave:  0
```

clients

Client	OpId	Locking	Waiting	SecsRunning	Op	Namespace	Query	client	msg	progress
initandlisten	11		{ waitingForLock: false }		2002	local.startup_log		0.0.0.0:0		
signalProcessingThread	0		{ waitingForLock: false }		0			:27017		
DataFileSync	1		{ waitingForLock: false }		0			:27017		
journal	3		{ waitingForLock: false }		0			:27017		
snapshotthread	5		{ waitingForLock: false }		0			:27017		
clientcursormon	6		{ waitingForLock: false }		0			:27017		
TTLMonitor	7		{ waitingForLock: false }		0			:27017		
RangeDeleter	8		{ waitingForLock: false }		0			:27017		
websvr	12		{ waitingForLock: false }		0			:27017		

dbtop (occurrences|percent of elapsed)

Understanding the reporting commands

The MongoDB engine provides useful management commands, which you can use to get a report from the current status of the databases or collections. In this section, you will learn how to execute and use these commands.

Executing a command

In order to execute a database command, you can use the `db.runCommand` function in the `mongo` interactive shell. To execute a command, you should pass the command name in the first parameter of the function.

The following code is an example of using this function:

```
db.runCommand("dbStats")
```

In the preceding example, `dbStats` is the name of a command.

Utilizing the dbStats command

The dbStats command is useful to get statistics from a database in a JSON document. Executing this command returns a short description about the number of collections, storage size, indexes on a database, average object or file size, and so on.

To run dbStats, you can use issue the following command:

```
db.runCommand("dbStats")
```

The following screenshot shows this command's output on a working database:

```
> db.runCommand("dbStats")
{
        "db" : "barkhat",
        "collections" : 8,
        "objects" : 250747,
        "avgObjSize" : 274.79226471303747,
        "dataSize" : 68903336,
        "storageSize" : 85983232,
        "numExtents" : 28,
        "indexes" : 8,
        "indexSize" : 36186976,
        "fileSize" : 469762048,
        "nsSizeMB" : 16,
        "dataFileVersion" : {
                "major" : 4,
                "minor" : 5
        },
        "extentFreeList" : {
                "num" : 0,
                "totalSize" : 0
        },
        "ok" : 1
}
```

Using this command enables you to get brief statistics of the current database or compare it with other databases.

Utilizing the collStats command

The output of this command is the same as the dbStats command. Executing the collStats command returns a collection's statistics, such as index size, number of records, average object size, and so on.

To execute the command, you should first select your database with the `use <dbname>` command and then issue following command:

```
db.<collection_name>.runCommand("collStats")
```

The following screenshot shows the output of the preceding command:

```
> db.posts.runCommand("collStats")
{
        "ns" : "barkhat.posts",
        "count" : 1435,
        "size" : 10561596,
        "avgObjSize" : 7359,
        "storageSize" : 17002496,
        "numExtents" : 5,
        "nindexes" : 1,
        "lastExtentSize" : 8101888,
        "paddingFactor" : 1,
        "systemFlags" : 1,
        "userFlags" : 0,
        "totalIndexSize" : 57232,
        "indexSizes" : {
                "_id_" : 57232
        },
        "ok" : 1
}
```

Use the preceding command to compare two or more collections' status on a database.

Understanding the serverStatus command

Another useful command to get a report from a database is the `serverStatus` command. This command represents a complete report from a database, collections, to the overall status of the database.

For instance, by issuing this command, you can check the uptime of a server and the server's local time, hostname, engine version, number of current active connections, and so on.

To use the `serverStatus` command after choosing the database, run the following command:

```
db.runCommand("serverStatus")
```

The following screenshot illustrates the output of the preceding command:

```
> db.runCommand("serverStatus")
{
        "host" : "mongotest",
        "version" : "2.6.0",
        "process" : "mongod",
        "pid" : NumberLong(1405),
        "uptime" : 17062,
        "uptimeMillis" : NumberLong(17061890),
        "uptimeEstimate" : 5364,
        "localTime" : ISODate("2014-05-22T20:30:00.883Z"),
        "asserts" : {
                "regular" : 0,
                "warning" : 0,
                "msg" : 0,
                "user" : 0,
                "rollovers" : 0
        },
        "backgroundFlushing" : {
                "flushes" : 98,
                "total_ms" : 562,
                "average_ms" : 5.73469387755102,
                "last_ms" : 7,
                "last_finished" : ISODate("2014-05-22T20:29:37.931Z")
        },
        "connections" : {
                "current" : 1,
                "available" : 203,
                "totalCreated" : NumberLong(3)
        },
        "cursors" : {
                "note" : "deprecated, use server status metrics",
                "clientCursors_size" : 0,
                "totalOpen" : 0,
                "pinned" : 0,
                "totalNoTimeout" : 0,
                "timedOut" : 0
        },
        "dur" : {
                "commits" : 29,
                "journaledMB" : 0,
```

This command is a shortcut to get a complete overview from a database or to compare the status of two databases.

Utilizing the replSetGetStatus command

If you are in a production environment with a replica set, this command is useful to find an overview of the replica set.

Using this command is as easy as issuing the following code:

```
db.runCommand("replSetGetStatus")
```

You can use the `replSetGetStatus` command to get a report about the replica set, the member's role, and the relationship between them or the replica set's configuration.

Using database logs

A MongoDB instance emits all database activities with log messages. According to the instance configuration, the database engine emits logs into a logfile or prints them in the console.

These log messages are useful when you face an issue with your database instance. You can read the logfiles and check the database. Most of the time, these log messages come in handy when you have trouble establishing and running a database instance.

There are a few options that you can use to control and manage logging for your database instance.

- `systemLog.quiet`: This is a Boolean value that defines the verbosity level of the MongoDB instance. The default value is `false`, and on setting this value to `true`, the log system doesn't record logs for the following actions:
  - The output of database commands
  - Replication
  - Connection accepted and closed

- `systemLog.path`: This is a string value that defines the path to save the logfile. By defining this value, you force the instance to emit the log messages into a file instead of returning them as a standard output.

  Please note that MongoDB overwrites logfiles by default after each restart of the database. You can change this option using the `systemLog.logAppend` option described in next section.

- `systemLog.logAppend`: This is a Boolean value, which is defined to append log messages to the existing file instead of overwriting logfiles. The value is `false` by default.

Consider the following configuration file:

```
dbpath = /usr/local/var/mongodb/
logpath = /var/log/mongodb.log
port = 27017
```

By using the preceding configuration file, the database engine emits logfiles into `/var/log/mongodb.log`, but it overwrites logfiles after each restart of the instance.

Furthermore, you can use the `mongod` or `mongos` command-line configuration like in the following command:

```
mongod --logpath /var/log/mongodb.log
```

The result of executing the preceding command is similar to the previous example with the configuration file.

In order to read the logfiles, you can use the `tail` or `cat` commands in Unix operating systems and text editors in Windows. For instance, in order to read the output of the previous example of logfile, you can issue the following command in a Unix operating system:

```
tail -f /var/log/mongodb.log
```

The output of the preceding command is as follows:

```
➜ /etc  tail -f /var/log/mongodb.log
2014-05-22T18:25:13.177+0430 [clientcursormon] connections:0
2014-05-22T18:30:13.281+0430 [clientcursormon] mem (MB) res:220 virt:9927
2014-05-22T18:30:13.281+0430 [clientcursormon]  mapped (incl journal view):7456
2014-05-22T18:30:13.282+0430 [clientcursormon] connections:0
2014-05-22T18:35:13.387+0430 [clientcursormon] mem (MB) res:220 virt:9927
2014-05-22T18:35:13.388+0430 [clientcursormon]  mapped (incl journal view):7456
2014-05-22T18:35:13.388+0430 [clientcursormon] connections:0
2014-05-22T18:40:13.482+0430 [clientcursormon] mem (MB) res:220 virt:9927
2014-05-22T18:40:13.483+0430 [clientcursormon]  mapped (incl journal view):7456
2014-05-22T18:40:13.483+0430 [clientcursormon] connections:0
```

Introducing web-based utilities

In this section, we will go through the web-based tools and utilities to manage and control the MongoDB instance. Tools in this category are generally easy to use and configure. Using a straightforward installation, you can configure the tools and then check the reports online using a web page or mobile application.

Utilizing the MMS monitoring service

MMS is a web-based tool provided by MongoDB to facilitate the process of deployment and management of MongoDB instance. You can access MMS at https://mms.mongodb.com/.

The following is a screenshot of the MMS monitoring service:

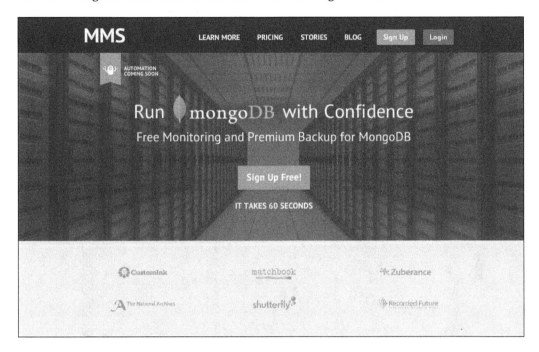

If you have a small MongoDB instance, you can use this tool for free. Moreover, to get more information about pricing, you can check the price list at https://mms. mongodb.com/pricing.

The MMS system supports all types of MongoDB instances, including standalone, sharded cluster, master/slave, and replica set.

The following list shows the main features of the MMS management tool:

- **Supports all MongoDB instances**: MMS supports all types of MongoDB instances, including **Sharded Cluster**, **Standalone**, **Replica Set**, and **Master/ Slave**. These options are shown in the following screenshot:

- **Backup strategy**: You can simply define your backup strategy and manage them via the web-based user interface. Furthermore, you are able to alter or add a plan whenever you want.

- **Customizable dashboard**: The dashboard section contains different charts and tables. You can arrange them in any order using its drag-and-drop feature.

- **Continuous backups and restorations**: MMS provides real-time and continuous backups with point-in-time recovery for both replica sets and sharded clusters.

- **User friendly and easy to use**: The usage of this tool is pretty simple and straightforward. All you need is to set up and configure your instance first.

- **Configurable alert messages**: Also, you can create alerts with different conditions and the system will send you notification messages via e-mail or SMS.

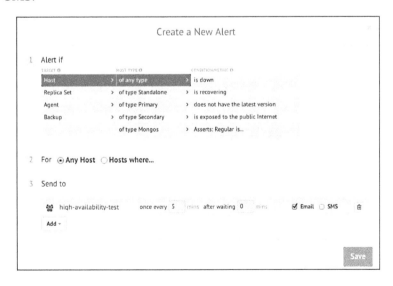

- **User/group management**: If you need to manage and control your MMS users or give them different privileges for different components, you can use the group and user management panel as shown in the following screenshot:

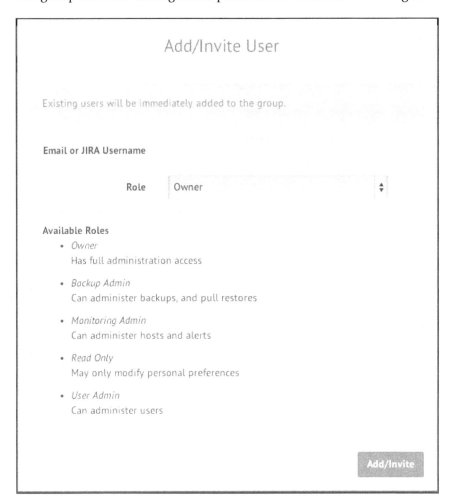

Understanding Scout

Scout is an enterprise-grade server monitoring tool. It is a web-based monitoring tool that provides different plugins to manage replica sets and configure alert messages.

In order to access the system, please visit `http://scoutapp.com`. The following screenshot shows the web page of Scout:

Unfortunately, Scout doesn't have any free plans, but you can try all plans for a limited period. You can find pricing and options at `https://scoutapp.com/subscriptions`.

The following list shows the advantages of using Scout as a management tool:

- **Easy to use**: Installing and using Scout is remarkably easy and straightforward. All you have to do is to install a package from gem and start the service. This is shown in the following screenshot:

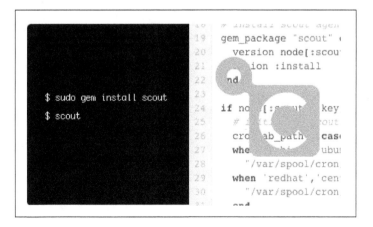

- **More than 70 plugins**: With more than 70 prepared plugins, you don't need to log in to your server by using SSH. You can simply use these plugins to arrange and control your server.

- **Writing custom plugin**: Another amazing feature of Scout is that you can write your custom plugin and install it in the Scout panel. The system provides a programming API, which you can use to expand your dashboard as shown in the following screenshot:

```
× load_averages.rb

1   class LoadAverages < Scout::Plugin
2     TEST_USAGE = "#{File.basename($0)} max_load
3
4     def build_report
5       if `uptime` =~ /load average(s*): ([\d.]
6         report :last_minute          => $2,
7                :last_five_minutes    => $4,
8                :last_fifteen_minutes => $6
9       else
10        raise "Unexpected output format"
11      end
```

- **Custom alerting system**: Scout supports a custom alerting system so that you can configure different alerts with your conditions. The system will send you a notification via e-mail or SMS.

- **E-mail and SMS notification**: It's important to receive downtime alert messages immediately. Scout supports both e-mail and SMS alerts.

Utilizing server density

Server density is an online management tool. Server density provides a module to manage MongoDB instances. It provides many useful features and by using Server density, you don't need to manage your server manually anymore.

In order to access server density, you can visit https://www.serverdensity.com/. This is shown in the following screenshot:

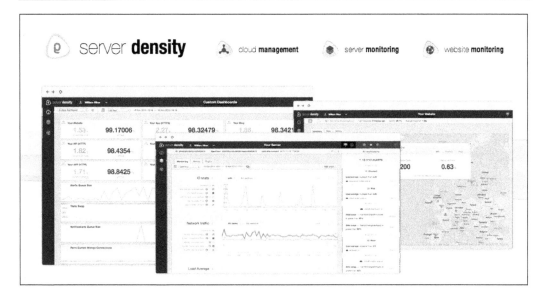

This service doesn't have any free plans, but you can request a trial version. You can check the price list at `https://www.serverdensity.com/pricing/`.

This service has some remarkable features that can help developers and administrators to manage the database effortlessly.

The following list shows these features:

- **Dashboard**: This service provides a complete MongoDB dashboard so you can monitor your server's status. This is shown in the following screenshot:

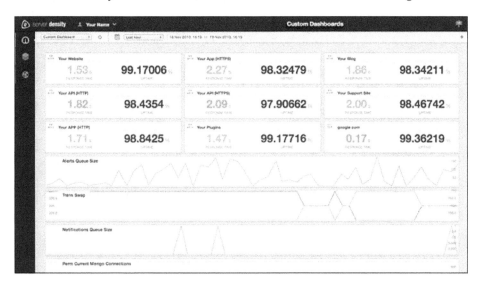

- **Plugins**: This service has a lot of useful plugins. You can install them in your dashboard with a simple mouse click. This feature is shown in the following screenshot:

- **Custom alert**: You can define alerts in server density and receive alerts using your e-mail or SMS in the same way as you receive for other services. Also, server density has mobile apps for iPhone and Android. Furthermore, you can use web hooks to get alerts via HTTP requests. This feature is demonstrated in the following screenshot:

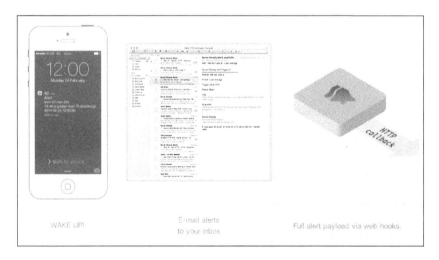

- **API**: Server density provides a current JSON API to use in almost all programming languages. You can develop your app and get the reports via this API. The following is a screenshot of HTTP JSON API:

HTTP JSON API - easy access from any language

Utilizing LogicMonitor

LogicMonitor is another useful web-based monitoring tool that supports different types of alerting systems.

LogicMonitor can be found at `http://lp.logicmonitor.com/`. The following is a screenshot of LogicMonitor:

The following list shows the main features of LogicMonitor:

- **Easy to manage and install**: This tool can be configured in a few straightforward steps, as shown in the following screenshot:

- **Alerting system**: This tool supports a full-featured alerting system and you can define your conditions to receive alert messages via SMS, e-mail, or phone call.

- **Dashboard**: This service provides a real-time dashboard with several components. You can arrange them in your order using its drag-and-drop system. The dashboard is shown in the following screenshot:

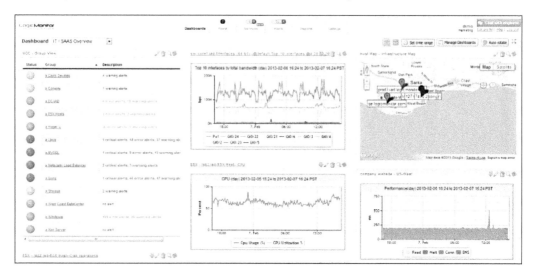

Unfortunately, there are no free plans to use this service. However, you can check the pricing at `http://www.logicmonitor.com/pricing/`.

Introducing FusionReactor

FusionReactor is a real-time management tool. It provides a plugin to manage database engines. Using this tool, you can manage your MongoDB instance in a simple manner.

In order to access this tool, visit `http://www.fusion-reactor.com/`. The home page of FusionReactor is shown in the following screenshot:

The major features of FusionReactor are as follows:

- **Real-time dashboard**: FusionReactor has a real-time dashboard with a lot of plugins. You can simply manage and arrange them in your required order. The following screenshot shows the dashboard of FusionReactor:

- **In-detail reports**: Using in-detail reports, you can view everything about your MongoDB instance.

FusionReactor doesn't offer any free plans, but you can check the pricing at `http://www.fusion-reactor.com/pricing/`.

 MongoDB has many other administration tools and you can find a detailed list by visiting `http://docs.mongodb.org/ecosystem/tools/administration-interfaces/`.

Introducing self-hosted utilities

There are many open source management utilities for MongoDB. You can download and install them on your machine. The following table shows the description and website for each of these tools:

Tool name	Description	Website
Robomongo	This is a shell-centric cross-platform MongoDB management tool.	`http://robomongo.org/`
mtop	`mtop` for MongoDB is a tool that is similar to `top`.	`https://github.com/beaufour/mtop`
Nagios	Nagios offers complete monitoring and alerting for servers, switches, applications, and services.	`http://www.nagios.org/`
Zabbix	This enterprise-class monitoring solution. This is a useful tool to monitor resources, servers' health and performance.	`http://www.zabbix.com/`
Motop	This is a real-time monitoring tool. It shows the current operations ordered by durations every second.	`https://github.com/tart/motop`
Ganglia	This is a scalable distributed monitoring system for high-performance computing systems.	`http://sourceforge.net/projects/ganglia/`
Munin	This is a networked monitoring tool to help analyze resource trends and problems.	`http://munin-monitoring.org/`
ManageEngine	This is a server and application performance monitoring tool that includes support for MongoDB.	`http://manageengine.com/products/applications_manager/help/monitors/mongodb-monitor.html`
MongoVUE	This is a MongoDB desktop application for Windows OS that gives you an elegant and user friendly GUI interface to work with MongoDB.	`http://www.mongovue.com/`

Summary

In this chapter, we introduced management and administration tools. Using these tools, you can ease the management process.

First of all, you learned all the major methods of managing a MongoDB instance, including profiling, using database logs, utilizing built-in management tools, and using web-based utilities to manage an instance.

Then, you learned how to work with the profiler in a database to diagnose and find slow operations. Then, you worked with built-in reporting tools such as `mongotop` or `mongostat`. These tools are easy to use and handy to monitor instance statistics.

Also, you studied how to use and execute database commands to get reports from active databases or collections. These commands are `dbStats`, `collStats`, and so on. Then, you learned how to use and read database logs to find issues in the running instances and diagnose it.

Moreover, you studied some web-based tools that are useful to easily manage a MongoDB instance remotely. You can now define your alerts or create a custom dashboard to watch available instances better.

Next, you introduced a list of open source tools. You can download and install the tools in this section on your machine and monitor your database instances. Most of them provide a good overview of instance statistics.

Index

Symbols

32-bit version of MongoDB
  limitations 21

A

advantages, Scout 133, 134
analytics methods 96
arbiter node
  about 30, 39, 47, 48
  URL 47
asynchronous replication 39

B

balancing process 70-72
benefits, sharding 67
bind_ip command 52
bsondump process 14
built-in reporting tools
  about 121
  mongostat 122
  mongotop 121, 122

C

chunks 24
clustering, in MongoDB
  about 27, 34
  configuration server 34
  mongos process, utilizing 34, 35
  query router, utilizing 34, 35
  shards 34
collStats command
  utilizing 124, 125

components, MongoDB
  core components 10
  diagnostic tools 16
  File storage (GridFS) tools 19
  import and export tools 13
  utilizing 9, 10
components, sharded cluster 68
concurrency
  URL, for information 25
configuration database 81
configuration, mongos instance 77, 78
configuration, replica set 51, 52
configuration server
  about 34, 68
  implementing 75-77
configuration server failure
  sharding 23, 24
core components, MongoDB
  data tools 15
  mongod 10, 11

D

database command
  executing 123
database diagnosing 118
database locks 24, 25
database logs
  using 127, 128
database monitoring 118
database profiler
  URL, for information 121
database profiler engine
  about 95
  URL, for information 95

Thank you for buying
MongoDB High Availability

About Packt Publishing

Packt, pronounced 'packed', published its first book *"Mastering phpMyAdmin for Effective MySQL Management"* in April 2004 and subsequently continued to specialize in publishing highly focused books on specific technologies and solutions.

Our books and publications share the experiences of your fellow IT professionals in adapting and customizing today's systems, applications, and frameworks. Our solution based books give you the knowledge and power to customize the software and technologies you're using to get the job done. Packt books are more specific and less general than the IT books you have seen in the past. Our unique business model allows us to bring you more focused information, giving you more of what you need to know, and less of what you don't.

Packt is a modern, yet unique publishing company, which focuses on producing quality, cutting-edge books for communities of developers, administrators, and newbies alike. For more information, please visit our website: www.packtpub.com.

About Packt Open Source

In 2010, Packt launched two new brands, Packt Open Source and Packt Enterprise, in order to continue its focus on specialization. This book is part of the Packt Open Source brand, home to books published on software built around Open Source licenses, and offering information to anybody from advanced developers to budding web designers. The Open Source brand also runs Packt's Open Source Royalty Scheme, by which Packt gives a royalty to each Open Source project about whose software a book is sold.

Writing for Packt

We welcome all inquiries from people who are interested in authoring. Book proposals should be sent to author@packtpub.com. If your book idea is still at an early stage and you would like to discuss it first before writing a formal book proposal, contact us; one of our commissioning editors will get in touch with you.

We're not just looking for published authors; if you have strong technical skills but no writing experience, our experienced editors can help you develop a writing career, or simply get some additional reward for your expertise.

Pentaho Analytics for MongoDB

ISBN: 978-1-78216-835-5   Paperback: 146 pages

Combine Pentaho Analytics and MongoDB to create powerful analysis and reporting solutions

1. This is a step-by-step guide that will have you quickly creating eye-catching data visualizations.

2. Includes a sample MongoDB database of web clickstream events for learning how to model and query MongoDB data.

3. Full of tips, images, and exercises that cover the Pentaho development lifecycle.

Ruby and MongoDB Web Development Beginner's Guide

ISBN: 978-1-84951-502-3   Paperback: 332 pages

Create dynamic web applications by combining the power of Ruby and MongoDB

1. Step-by-step instructions and practical examples to creating web applications with Ruby and MongoDB.

2. Learn to design the object model in a NoSQL way.

3. Create objects in Ruby and map them to MongoDB.

Please check **www.PacktPub.com** for information on our titles

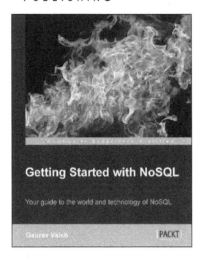

Getting Started with NoSQL

ISBN: 978-1-84969-498-8   Paperback: 142 pages

Your guide to the world and technology of NoSQL

1. First hand, detailed information about NoSQL technology.

2. Learn the differences between NoSQL and RDBMS and where each is useful.

3. Understand the various data models for NoSQL.

4. Compare and contrast some of the popular NoSQL databases on the market.

Instant MongoDB

ISBN: 978-1-78216-970-3   Paperback: 72 pages

Get up to speed with one of the world's most popular NoSQL database

1. Learn something new in an Instant! A short, fast, focused guide delivering immediate results.

2. Query in MongoDB from the Mongo shell.

3. Learn about the aggregation framework and Map Reduce support in Mongo.

4. Tips and tricks for schema designing and how to develop high performance applications using MongoDB.

www.ingramcontent.com/pod-product-compliance
Lightning Source LLC
LaVergne TN
LVHW081344050326
832903LV00024B/1308